Enter by the Gate

Enter by the Gate

Jesus' 7 Guidelines When Making Hard Choices

Flora Slosson Wuellner

UPPER
ROOM BOOKS®
NASHVILLE

The Upper Room® Web site: www.upperroom.org

UPPER ROOM®, UPPER ROOM BOOKS® and design logos are trade-
marks owned by The Upper Room®, Nashville, Tennessee. All rights
reserved.

Scripture quotations not otherwise identified are from the New Revised
Standard Version of the Bible © 1989, Division of Christian Education of
the National Council of the Churches of Christ in the United States of
America. Used by permission. All rights reserved.

Scripture noted NIV is taken from the *Holy Bible, New International
Version. NIV.* Copyright 1973, 1978, 1984 by International Bible Society.
Used by permission of Zondervan. All rights reserved.

Scripture noted AP is author's paraphrase.

"They Cast Their Nets in Galilee" © William A. Percy, 1885–1942. Used by
permission of Leroy P. Percy.

Cover Design: Gore Studio, Nashville
Cover Photo: Index Stock
First printing: 2004

Library of Congress Cataloging-in-Publication Data

Wuellner, Flora Slosson.
  Enter by the gate : Jesus' 7 guidelines when making hard choices / by
Flora Slosson Wuellner.
    p. cm.
  ISBN 0-8358-9883-0
  1. Christian life. I. Title.
  BV4501.3.W84 2004
  248.4—dc22   2004011371

Printed in the United States of America

This book is dedicated with love and celebration
to seven shining stars in my life:
Paul, Luke, Flora, Charlotte, John, Alexander, Carmen

They shall mount up with wings like eagles,
they shall run and not be weary,
they shall walk and not faint.
—Isaiah 40:31

Contents

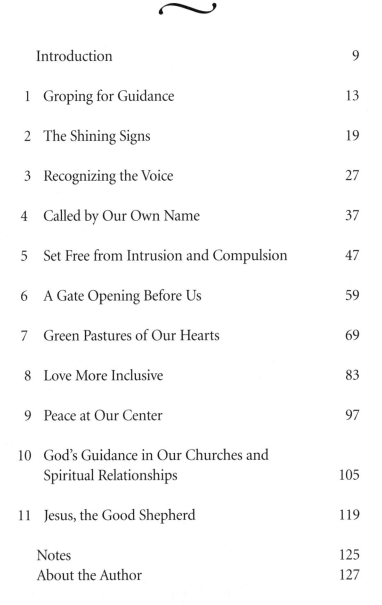

Introduction

$\mathcal{M}$y experience is that the possibilities for self-deception are enormous and frightening, even for sincerely devoted Christians," a respected church leader recently wrote to me.

I could only agree. The search for guidance, whether as individuals or as communities, is threatened with potential disaster. Each of us, as we face our hard choices, is aware that our relationships, our daily work, our commitments, our happiness and health, the way we relate to the world around us, our very lives, depend on the source of our guidance.

The damage done by misguidance or abusive guidance can be devastating for our personal lives. Far more devastating is misguidance that affects whole communities. Instant global communication, demand for swift decisions that affect millions, and sophisticated means of manipulating public opinion, all make the need for healthy, dependable guidance ever more urgent.

A wise, elderly statesman once said to me, "We have come such a long way in human rights, gender and ethnic equality, ecological awareness, concern for peace [since] I was born ninety years ago. In spite of all our problems, the change is almost unbelievable. But though we are in many ways better, we are also more in danger. Our choices now can so quickly become destructive to so many, more than at any other time in human history."

Our churches face serious mistakes no less than secular institutions. We who claim to be under God's guidance often grope blindly or surrender to false ideologies and predatory agendas masquerading as God's will.

' Misleading guidance also arises from *within* us. Whether within individuals, family groups, workplaces, political parties, churches, neighborhoods, or nations, unhealed infected wounds of hurt, fear, anger, and guilt often pass as God's voice. Our rigid traditions and our pride of entitlement often go by the name of righteousness. Even when most sincere, we are nevertheless frequently misled. How do we hear God's authentic voice? How do we recognize God's guidance in our individual hearts and lives as well as in the communities around us?

Every word and act of Jesus radiated God's love and guidance, but a story in John's Gospel, chapter 10, encapsulates powerful implications for our search for guidance. Jesus tells a vivid story about a flock of sheep who recognize the voice and presence of their true shepherd over against the misleading voices of strangers, deceivers, and predators. We are told that the true shepherd enters by the gate. What is the valid gate of God's guidance? What are the authentic signs of the One who comes to us through the gate? I see seven basic guidelines for recognizing this guidance.

John's Gospel comes to us from a different perspective than

that of the other three Gospels. Researchers are still unclear just who wrote it and when. Was it a very early or very late document? Was it written by John the apostle or written in his name by one of his followers? In any case it is obvious that the author was intimately close to Jesus' heart and inner spiritual life. Even more than in the synoptic Gospels, the oneness between God and Jesus is manifest. In this Gospel, what Jesus says and what God says flow forth as one voice.

In this story of mutual recognition and bonding between shepherd and sheep we sense God's own self speaking to us, revealing the authentic signs of God's guidance, as well as the warning signs of the misleaders.

This book will not arrogantly promise that all questions will be answered instantly, that we will never make mistakes, or that no risk is involved in our choices, even when sensitive to God's shining signs of guidance. This book will not provide rigid, legalistic formulas. Rather I have tried to reflect on the transforming relationship between ourselves and God the Beloved. It is from the deep bond of love that the signs and guidelines rise.

You will find suggested reflections and meditations at the close of each chapter. You may enter the meditations immediately or read the book through and then return to the meditations. These are offered as suggestions, not rules. The only authority exists between God and your own heart. Change any wording or imagery to be more helpful to you.

Give this same freedom and permission to others you may be guiding, whether in a one-to-one relationship or in a group setting. Be clear that each person is free to choose other words or imagery, to leave the meditation altogether, to reflect or pray in some other way.

Introduction

Only in the spirit of Jesus Christ's own freedom do we help one another and ourselves to move into the adventure of the shining signs and through the authentic gate of guidance.

Groping for Guidance

When he saw the crowds, he had compassion for them, because they were harassed and helpless, like sheep without a shepherd.

—Matthew 9:36

We grope for true guidance. We search for God's answer in our choices. Our questions and decisions are urgent.

"Should I stay in this relationship? I see signs of abusiveness, but I did promise faithfulness, and I would feel lonely . . ."

"The job pays well and my family needs the money, but I feel so restless. All my life I have wanted to . . ."

"They are urging this new medical treatment on me, but I just don't know. Something doesn't feel quite right . . ."

"This project is so important for everybody. Isn't it God's will that I should put everything else on the back burner?"

"Should we invite her to live with us? She needs help, but we are so crowded and I get so tired. Maybe this is my cross . . ."

"If I publish the truth and give the evidence, a lot of people are going to be hurt. Maybe I should forget about it or just delay . . ."

"O send out your light and your truth; let them lead me" was the cry of the psalmist three thousand years ago (Ps. 43:3). For some of us it is a daily, hourly cry. What is God's will? How can we tell we are on the right path?

Sometimes we are told just to do our duty, listen to our conscience. But some of history's worst crimes (including Jesus' crucifixion) were committed by people who thought they were doing their duty. Others often foist their agendas and ideologies on us as our duty. Our conscience may be formed by the rigid expectations of others. How can we discern our *real* duty?

Obey the Bible? The Bible is our foundational vision of God. God reaches to us through the depth and thrust of scripture. The face of God is increasingly revealed to us through scripture. But we cannot deny that sincere men and women, all searching the same Bible, derive different interpretations of what the Bible says about war, economics, ethnic and gender equality, family relationships, ways to govern a church, and so on. Neither can we deny that several times Jesus challenged certain parts of earlier scriptures, *not* (he makes clear) to destroy the guidance of scripture but to fulfill its deep and central meaning (see Matt. 5:17-18, 21-22, 27-28). Who can we choose as guides to the authentic meaning of scripture as we face our choices?

Obey our church laws and leaders? Church laws change through the centuries. Which are valid? Church leaders are human and fallible, and their mistakes can be disastrous.

Put others first and ourselves last? For individuals caught in abusive relationships, no advice is more dangerous. They are all too easily persuaded to view victimhood as unselfishness. Where can we find guidance about remaining in relationships? Who will help us set borders and limits?

Trust our intuition? How do we distinguish between genuine intuition and old habits of emotional response rising from unhealed hurts, inner anxieties, or sudden irresponsible impulses? Often these emotional habits masquerade as God's guidance.

Be guided by those who love us? Yes, if those who love us know how to hear us and respond to us without projecting their own agendas and personal expectations on us. If Jesus had let himself be guided by his family, he certainly never would have left Nazareth. His family thought he was out of his mind!

Should we then abandon these traditional guidelines? Certainly not. God speaks to us through them as well as through other ways. The problem we face is that *other* voices, pressures, and urgings speak to us in these same time-honored guidelines.

Once our family had a little kitchen radio that would switch channels mysteriously at times. We would tune in to one program and after a few minutes realize we were hearing something else altogether.

"It is some kind of interference with the channel reception," the repairman told us. "Either you or something else gets in the way of the proper wavelength." Quite so. Talk about a metaphor! Jesus would have loved it. Often I have opened myself to God's guidance, made a choice, and then later realized that somehow my channel had switched without my knowing it. The interference may have been someone else's plan projected on me. Or I myself may have inwardly switched over to an unhealed conflict, habit of thought, or impulsive bright idea within me.

Where do we turn for the authentic signs of guidance? Jesus told a story about this dilemma. As we read it carefully and reflect on it prayerfully, we begin to see the shining signs.

Reflection and Meditation

O send out your light and your truth;
    let them lead me.

—Psalm 43:3

Choose a comfortable, restful posture. God's limitless love and strength undergird and hold you. God already knows your question, your problem, your longing and confusion. God longs to help and guide you. The *will of God* (from both Greek and Hebrew) means the deep desire of God, the longing of God.

Take a few deep, slow, gentle breaths without pushing or forcing. Then breathe naturally and peacefully. Think of each breath as God's own life of renewal flowing into you. Picture or just think of this breath of life flowing into all parts of your body, especially to bodily areas that feel stressed, tight, or tense. Let these bodily areas breathe the breath of life.

When you feel ready, ask yourself:

How have I looked for God's guidance in the past? through prayer? through my church? through other people's opinions? through my conscience? through intuitive inner feelings? Or did guidance come in other ways to me: through a book, a dream, a walk in the woods, a clear sense of authentic duty? Or did it come in some other way?

How did I feel when this guidance came? Surprised? Pushed? Peaceful? Anxious? Renewed and strengthened?

Think of some decisions you made based on the guidance

you felt. Ask yourself: Did those decisions turn out to be the right choices? If so, what were the results of my choices?

If not, what misled me? Was it the influence of others? Some problem within me? Did I overlook warning signs?

What question or problem am I facing now? How do I feel about the choices I am encountering?

Breathe again with a few slow, deep breaths and then breathe naturally. Let your body rest.

When ready, express your problem as clearly as possible to God and to yourself in your own way, using your own words. You do not yet know the right answer, but God does. You will be given authentic signs in the right time.

Picture or just think of the question enfolded in God's light or resting in God's heart. It may help to think of Jesus holding your question in his hands.

Rest quietly. If anxious feelings rise, that is natural. Just share the feeling with God without guilt. Let the feeling also be enfolded by God's light. When you feel ready, breathe a few deep, slow breaths and gradually leave your meditation, gently massaging your face and hands.

The Shining Signs

~

*L*et us hear Jesus' story of guidance as given in John's Gospel:

Very truly, I tell you, anyone who does not enter the sheepfold by the gate, but climbs in by another way is a thief and a bandit. The one who enters by the gate is the shepherd of the sheep. The gatekeeper opens the gate for him, and the sheep hear his voice. He calls his own sheep by name and leads them out. When he has brought out all his own, he goes ahead of them, and the sheep follow him because they know his voice. They will not follow a stranger, but they will run from him because they do not know the voice of strangers. . . . Very truly, I tell you, I am the gate for the sheep. All who came before me are thieves and bandits; but the sheep did not listen to them. I am the gate. Whoever enters by me will be saved, and will come in and go out and find pasture. The thief comes only to steal and kill and destroy. I came that they may have life, and have it abundantly.

Chapter Two

I am the good shepherd. The good shepherd lays down his life for the sheep. The hired hand, who is not the shepherd and does not own the sheep, sees the wolf coming and leaves the sheep and runs away—and the wolf snatches them and scatters them. . . . I am the good shepherd. I know my own and my own know me. . . . I have other sheep that do not belong to this fold. I must bring them also, and they will listen to my voice. So there will be one flock, one shepherd. . . . I give them eternal life, and they will never perish. No one will snatch them out of my hand" (John 10:1-5, 7-12, 14, 16, 28).

Had Jesus been a shepherd as well as a carpenter in his youth? Many of his most poignant and powerful stories and metaphors center around the relationship of the shepherd and the sheep.

In biblical times, sheep were a major source of wealth for a family, tribe, or town. They were valued mainly for their wool and milk products. Only occasionally were they used for food since just the very wealthy could afford to eat meat often. Sheep were considered the most acceptable animals for sacrifice in the Temple in Jerusalem; therefore, special flocks were raised for that purpose.

But there is much more to Jesus' stories about sheep than the animals' economic, household, or sacrificial value. We find in these stories a tenderness, a caring, a powerful guidance, a deep trusting relationship between sheep and the true shepherd. The awareness of this relationship was not a new idea of course. Throughout scripture we often find God compared to a deeply caring, authentic shepherd. The comparison is surprising because people often considered a full-time shepherd to be an uncouth, unorthodox person. A shepherd could not observe all the sabbath laws or the strict laws of ritual cleanliness. The well-being of the sheep, night and day, had to come first.

In this particular story in John's Gospel, we are asked first to picture a village at night, with the sheep penned together in a communal walled enclosure. Since each household could not afford to build a separate strong sheepfold, the villagers built one for everybody's sheep. The walls of the enclosure were built of sturdy wood, stones, brick, or sometimes thick barricades of thornbushes to defend against the constant danger of thieves, wolves, and mountain lions.

There would be only one entrance to the sheep pen, closed by a gate and usually watched over by a guard, a gatekeeper. At night this gatekeeper would lie down by the entrance so no one could leave or enter without stepping on his body. The gatekeeper knew the times at dawn or just before dawn when the shepherds customarily would arrive to call out their sheep. Anyone coming *before* that time probably was a thief, intending to steal what sheep he could.

The shepherd or a trusted family member (male or female) would have to be recognized first by the gatekeeper, who would open the gate for him or her. The sheep would also need to recognize their own shepherd. Each shepherd had his or her own special call, song, whistle, or other sound that the sheep knew. The sheep would come to their shepherd, ignoring other voices and calls.

As the sheep came one by one out of the enclosure, the shepherd would count them, usually touch each one, and perhaps speak its name. A shepherd who cherished his sheep had a special name for each one. Then the sheep would be led out of the crowded, smelly, communal enclosure to head for the grasslands. They might be gone for a day or perhaps for weeks, depending on the time of year, the weather, and the location of the best pastures. Often the shepherd had to guide them through rocky, dangerous wilderness to reach the fresh grass and clean water high in the hills.

During my student pastorates in the Rocky Mountain area, I often saw flocks of sheep being guided high into the foothill pastures, where they would stay for the short summer, guarded by one or two shepherds. In biblical times a hired hand, a transient day laborer, might accompany a shepherd to assist in the work. Usually this hired person would not be given total responsibility for the flock, for he could not be trusted to put the sheep ahead of his own safety in case of emergencies.

In the Near East, shepherds still walk ahead of the sheep, leading them, not behind pushing or goading them. The shepherd prepares the way, watches for dangerous paths, steep ravines, poisonous weeds, or threat of predators.

Even when settled in green pastures, the shepherd of biblical times was always alert for accidents, sickness, sores, parasites, as well as sheep who wandered off and got lost. The shepherds also watched for abuse among the sheep themselves, making sure that the strong ones did not hurt or bully the vulnerable sheep or push them aside from the fresh water and grass.

We who live in cities may find it hard to translate this special bond between shepherd and sheep into recognizable modern equivalents. We will understand the meaningful heart to the story, however, if we think how we have felt when we cared lovingly for children, old people, the sick, or those with special needs. If we have watched over and guided a class of students, supervised an office staff, guided a parish, counseled clients, cared about customers, tended a home and garden, shouldered responsibility for a neighborhood, a city, a church, a nation—we will understand.

However, the unique aspect of this story is not just the loving care of shepherd for the flock. Psalm 23, which we all love, covers most of those caring, nurturing aspects in an incomparable way. This story in John's Gospel focuses on the *recognition* of the true shepherd by the sheep: the way they know the authentic presence and voice, how they recognize the special signs of their own true shepherd. This is a story primarily of *discernment*: what to listen for, what to look for, whom to trust, whom to distrust, the quality and results of the true shepherd's leadership.

As I reflect on this story, I see seven major guiding signs. These guidelines have deep implications for our choices, our ethical decisions, our own awareness of the quality and nature of God's guidance as we choose which path to take and discern whether to continue on that path.

1. Do we recognize the voice that guides us, its special quality and characteristics?

2. Are we "called by name" as unique persons or treated only as part of a general category?

3. Are we set free from intrusion and compulsion as we make our choices? Are we shown how to recognize those who would trespass and force us into certain decisions?

4. Are gates opening before us in practical and specific ways?

5. Are we experiencing renewal, inner healing, and sustaining nurture while on our path? Are there actual pastures as well as perils in our lives?

6. Are we growing in the ability to love not only deeply and compassionately but also inclusively, welcoming the alien and the outcast?

7. Are we experiencing the still point of inner peace in the midst of risk, turmoil, and conflict?

As we begin the adventure of the shining signs, the journey through the valid gates of guidance, let us explore the living relationship with the Shepherd that is the root, core, and meaning of all the other signs.

Reflection and Meditation

Relax your body in whatever way works best for you. Take a few slow, deep breaths, then relax your breathing. God the Shepherd is with you now, even if you feel nothing in particular.

Slowly reread Jesus' story in John 10. What aspect of the story especially interests you, draws you? Focus on those verses. How do you feel about the passage?

Can you picture or feel yourself as a part of this story? Where do you find yourself in the story? Are you resting in the enclosure with others near you during the night? Or do you feel like the gatekeeper—watchful, responsible, resting by the entrance? Do you hear a call at dawn indicating the shepherd is coming? Do you recognize something in that call or that presence?

Or are you at the point where you are ready to leave the enclosure and go out through the gate? Are you already on the trail? Are you in the pasture?

Is there anything about this story that troubles you? Tell

God what you feel. What main question rises within you at this point?

Do you wish to write down your thoughts? Draw? Dance the story? Focus quietly on a word or central image in the story? If you have no special feeling about the story, do not push or force a reaction. Just rest, breathing in God's presence and breath of life.

When you feel ready, stretch, gently massage your face and hands, and with quietness leave your meditation.

Recognizing the Voice

~

The one who enters by the gate is the shepherd of the sheep. The gatekeeper opens the gate for him, and the sheep hear his voice . . . they know his voice.

—John 10:2-4

Who stands at our gate and claims to be our guide? What quality of voice do we hear? What are the guide's characteristics?

My inner gatekeeper has not always been wise and alert. My inner gatekeeper has sometimes welcomed guidance and influences that were not the authentic Shepherd.

In my early twenties, longing for a spirituality that would take me deeper into God than the usual forms of organized religion, I joined a spiritual training group. Their teachings seemed so wise, so beautiful. For several months I hungrily ingested their teachings and guidance toward a God-filled life.

At last, I told myself, *I am learning true spirituality. At last I am learning what God desires from us.* I kept telling myself this for many weeks as I was continually though gently reproved for my thoughts, my feelings, my reactions, my longings, indeed, for my very personality.

"God is not interested (nor are we) in your human personality," I was told. "All God cares about is our divine potentiality. The self must die. The self is only an illusion, a block to divine perception. You must drop your defenses and abandon your former concepts. Don't react to things with your own feelings and ideas. Become like a clear dewdrop, reflecting only God."

This seemed so holy. Earnestly I worked and prayed (with total lack of success) to become a clear dewdrop. I tried to banish all the coloring of my own personality, all spontaneity. It took a severe emotional shock to make me realize that this outwardly gentle spiritual community was systematically and powerfully destroying my sense of self-worth, my confidence, my whole spontaneous individuality. Fortunately I was guided to several spiritually robust theologians outside this community who understood the meaning of the Incarnation.

With their help I realized that God created and honors our human condition, that God cares about our thoughts and feelings, that our natural emotional responses are part of our healthy spiritual lives, often to be healed but never obliterated. I was excited to learn that God did not want to turn me into a transparent dewdrop or colorless glass. I vividly recall pacing up and down a long hallway, clutching a book by the great Martin Buber, mumbling to myself, "So God really *does* love me as a natural, spontaneous human being!"

After this experience, I never forgot how quickly and insidiously the "stranger" can enter our gate and take over our life. I had not recognized the stranger in my gates because I did not know the identifying characteristics of the true Shepherd. I had thought anything "spiritual" by definition came from God.

As Christians, we believe that the words, the actions, and, above all, the personality of Jesus supremely reveal to us the nature, heart, and will of God. But how well do we know that personality? What are the distinguishing, recognizable signs of that personality? What was Jesus like when he walked the earth? What do we really see when we read the stories about him in the Gospels? Though these stories were written many centuries ago and not recorded in their present form until years after Jesus' death, a unique, intensely human and distinctive personality comes to us through the hearsay and mists of time. A personality bursts through the pages of the Bible and is with us now— powerful, gentle, uniquely himself.

What made Jesus joyful? What made him angry? When did he cry? When did he feast? What moved him to compassion? Did he have a sense of humor? What questions did he ask? When did he act swiftly? When did he pause? Did he love beauty? What were his prayers like? Did he ever let other people help him? Did he ever change his mind? Was he sometimes afraid? How did he relate to children, to women, to enemies, to strangers? Did he notice the little everyday things? How did he handle interruptions and surprises?

We know these things about family and friends. Why do we seldom ask such questions about our eternal friend and guide? Do we lack curiosity or reverence? Do we assume Jesus was not quite human because he was so deeply united with God?

Learning the distinguishing characteristics of this most warmly human as well as God-filled personality is a priority for us. We learn about Jesus not in order to imitate him. I doubt if we could. What would it mean to imitate Jesus in a medical decision, for example? How would imitation help us decide who to marry or what job or project to choose? Jesus came for a far more radically transforming purpose than merely to serve as a role model. Jesus came to invite us into a living relationship with him, to abide, live, and move in his spirit, as the branch abides in the living vine. Just as the bird does not imitate the air or the fish imitate the water but rather *abide* in their life-giving element, so are we to live in Jesus and Jesus live in us (John 15:4-5). Out of this transforming relationship we can form our decisions—not by imitation but by the unfolding of Jesus' spirit in this time and place in our lives.

Jesus is not limited to the stories written about him in the Bible. They are our touchstone, the foundational revealing of this incredible personality. Martin Luther said, "The Bible is the *cradle* of Christ, the living Word." Jesus is alive and active in our own stories today. What is Jesus doing through us now? How is Jesus affecting us at this moment? John closes his Gospel with these provocative words:

> But there are also many other things that Jesus did; if every one of them were written down, I suppose that the world itself could not contain the books that would be written (John 21:25).

Are we these books? Is every Christian a book of Acts in which Jesus speaks, heals, transforms? I believe so. We become living books about Jesus. Soon we begin to sense the quality, the characteristics, the *feel* of his personality, in much the same way we often sense the giver of the gift before we look at the tag or know who wrote the letter before we look at the signature.

As this awareness of the characteristics of Jesus' personality deepens, we also sense when it is a "stranger" at our gate rather than the true Shepherd. If we sense coercion, spiritual or emotional abuse, arrogance, contempt for self or others, rigidity or alienation, we will know that whatever that spirit is, it is not the spirit of Jesus Christ.

False images of Jesus—the vapid, sentimental ones or the coercive, controlling prisons of the spirit often thrust upon us in Jesus' name—do not represent the true spirit of Jesus. I meet many people who have been seriously wounded by the emotional, spiritual cruelties, coercions, and manipulations committed in the name of the very one who came to set us free and give us life abundant.

Once I visited a small church led by a woman of magnetic eloquence. I had heard wonderful things about her. In the middle of the service, my daughter whispered to me, "Why are your hands trembling?" Startled, I realized she was right: my hands were trembling. Why? The atmosphere was charged with tension and anxiety. I began to observe how this pastor used power over her submissive congregation. She used scripture out of context in threatening ways. She singled out individual members for public rebuke and shaming. She asked little children to come forward and told them "lovingly" how misunderstood they were, how wrong their parents were.

After the service I left the church as quickly as possible. I did not want to meet this woman personally or even to touch her hand. Later I learned more details of the total control she exerted over the lives of church members. She decided whether they were allowed medical treatment, whether they could go to college, whether they could attend family reunions, how they should cook and eat. All this she did in the name of Jesus.

We need to read scripture itself in the light of the eyes and heart of Jesus. Parts of the Bible present God as a vengeful destroyer. Some passages depict God as requiring the faithful to destroy others. In these passages the clouds of human misunderstanding have temporarily covered the sun of God's true nature. This awareness makes us uneasy. If our human fears and hatreds can be projected on God even in scripture, what can we depend on? We need to remember that Jesus, well aware of this problem, challenged certain parts of scripture which he believed cast a shadow on the *true* revelation of God through scripture (see Matt. 5:38-45). I believe that anything in scripture that denies or falls short of Jesus' heart and vision is not God's authentic word. A human writer or a traditional, rigid communal mindset got in the way of God's message.

As we increasingly abide in Jesus Christ, live in that heart, see through those eyes, we begin to notice a strange paradox. We the sheep begin to take on the nature of the Shepherd! Every metaphor and parable has its limits, and this story in John 10 puts us in the role of sheep. Sheep are not notable for their charm or intelligence. They are singularly clueless. They wander off and get lost. They eat poisonous weeds. They fall into ravines. They graze at the same spot until they strip it of all grass and pollute the ground. (Actually, this *does* sound a lot like us humans!) At best sheep are neither exciting nor creative. Is this really the way God sees us? Does God want us to be, at best, submissive sheep?

Not at all. Jesus told many other stories that reveal humans as complex and potentially creative sons and daughters of God.

We are not just to be obedient animals for all eternity. This story centers on the deep love, the trust, the bond, and the discerning recognition of the characteristics of the shepherd. This particular story does not emphasize the tremendous paradoxical truth that we the sheep *change*. In our shepherding role to others— as parent, teacher, caregiver, counselor, listening friend—we begin to guide as we have been guided. Our faces and voices will change. The way we listen and respond will change, not through imitation but spontaneously through deep love. "When he is revealed, we will be like him, for we will see him as he is" (1 John 3:2).

A powerful way to pray when we find ourselves in a shepherding role would be something like this: "Living Christ, Shepherd of our lives, enfold me in your spirit, speak through my voice, touch through my hands. Give me your listening heart, the power of your silences, the compassion of your words. Let me be transformed and guided by you, even as I am helping to guide others."

We can pray such a prayer (in our own words, of course) when we are talking with someone; counseling; leading a group; teaching a class; chairing a meeting, organizing a program; writing a letter, an e-mail, a book, an article; or just chatting with someone on a plane or bus who needs a listening ear.

Let us explore further the shining signs of the true Shepherd, the guiding presence.

Reflection and Meditation

I am the good shepherd. I know my own and my own know me.

—JOHN 10:14

Relax your body in whatever way is best for you. Take a few deep, slow breaths and then breathe naturally. Remember you are undergirded and enfolded by God's strong love.

When you feel ready, start thinking about the living Jesus Christ. How do you really feel about this person?

Do you believe he is just a great historical figure or a person still alive?

Is he a presence in your life in a way that feels real to you? If so, how would you picture him?

Is there anything about the thought of Jesus that makes you feel uneasy or that is wounding to you? Some old memory or association? Or the way he is so often represented in church, in art, in movies? Be honest in this reflection. God already knows how you feel and is not offended. God wants to help you understand your feelings and responses.

Are there some traditional ways of presenting Jesus that trouble you? Try to discern what bothers you about them.

What is there about Jesus that would make you wish to be his friend?

What is it about Jesus that makes you think of God?

If Jesus were sitting next to you now, what would you want to say, to share, to ask?

Jesus told us, "Remember, I am with you always" (Matt. 2:20). If you feel ready (you may wish to come back to this later), claim his actual presence near you now in any form that feels authentic to you: healing hands; a man in a long white robe; a presence of light; an inner word; a strong, living tree or vital fruitful vine; a gentle but powerful animal form (such as C. S. Lewis's lion, Aslan); a healing, loving person in your life; or in some other form.

What is the special feeling, the quality of this presence? Is there a word that summarizes this presence, such as *healing, compassion, joy, welcome, light, warmth, release, clear strength, safety, transforming challenge*? Another word?

Would you recognize the quality and characteristics of this presence when it is actually with you? Would you sense its absence? its opposite?

When you feel ready, talk to this presence, whether inwardly or aloud. Express your need, your question, your feeling, in your own words.

Sit quietly in the presence. Breathe slowly and deeply, then naturally. This presence of the living Jesus Christ will remain with you. You can turn at any moment to that presence with any problem, any feeling.

Stretch; gently massage your face and hands. Quietly leave your meditation.

Called by Our Own Name

~

He calls his own sheep by name.

—John 10:3

I met a world-known spiritual leader once, whose handclasp was limp, whose eyes wandered around the room never focusing on our faces, who never spoke our names. We were not there for him. It was hard to feel God's presence through him.

When God guides us, the guidance is always personal and always focuses on our own personal problem. In Jesus' story, he tells us that each sheep in the fold had its own name, and the shepherd spoke each name. Each sheep was special, at least to its true shepherd.

I have learned to be suspicious of any guidance that treats us impersonally as part of a category, as a case, as just one aspect of a generality. No matter how holy or idealistic, guidance that gives the same answer to everybody, ignoring individual needs and individual differences is questionable to me.

A caring shepherd would always note the characteristics and the special needs of each sheep: This is the timid one who must be led gently. This is the assertive, bold one who responds best to tough love. This one needs to be touched, held, talked to. That one likes to be let alone to try things out. The one over there stumbles easily, has sensitive skin, and bruises easily. This ewe, about to give birth, is tired. That old ram over there thinks he is stronger than he really is. Here is a born leader; others instinctively follow her. He lags behind, munching, and often wanders off, getting lost. She is still sensitive from her wound, still needs healing.

God knows each of us personally: our special gifts, needs, hurts, and problems. Significantly, in the Gospels, Jesus never gives the same specific guidance for everybody. We read that no matter what he is doing, when a person comes to him with a need or question (often an *unspoken* need or question), Jesus gives full attention to that person. He shapes his guidance to the specific problem and special need of that person.

"Follow me," he tells Peter (Matt. 4:18-19).

"Go home to your friends, and tell them how much the Lord has done for you," he instructs the man he releases from demonic possession (Mark 5:19).

"Sell what you own and give the money to the poor," he advises the rich young ruler (Mark 10:21).

Zacchaeus is encouraged in his decision to give up half his money (Luke 19:8).

"Tell no one," he directs some whom he has healed (Matt. 8:14, AP).

"Show yourselves to the priests," he tells those healed of leprosy (Luke 17:14).

"Sell your cloaks and buy swords," he counsels the disciples at the Last Supper (Luke 22:36, AP).

"Put away your sword," he orders Peter in Gethsemane (John 18:11, AP). To the Roman centurion whose servant Jesus heals he never mentions swords at all (Matt. 8:5-13).

Are there no general guidelines that apply to all of us? Yes, the great undergirding guidance of Jesus is, "You shall love the Lord your God with all your heart, and with all your soul, and with all your mind, and with all your strength. . . . You shall love your neighbor as yourself" (Mark 12:30-31). This, he tells us, is the supreme heart and meaning of scripture, the supreme will of God. But we are left astonishingly free in how this guidance applies to individual choices, such as what job to take, whom to marry, where we should live, what medical treatment to pursue, how to budget money, what community projects to undertake.

This is the approach of a good physician or fitness trainer whose purpose is to heal, to help us toward wholeness. With each patient or client, a caring health professional will say, "Let's look at your personal health history, study your present condition and body type, and work out the plan best for *you.*" We must suspect guidance that diagnoses and prescribes according to agendas, preoccupations, and expectations of the adviser.

One of my dear friends wanted from childhood to be a nurse. She had the gifts, intelligence, gentleness, compassion, patience, alertness, attention to detail, warmth, genuine interest in others, and the ability to stick to a task until it was finished. Her mother had studied medicine as a young woman but had never finished her medical degree. When my friend shared her dream of nursing, the mother immediately threw her weight against the plan.

"No daughter of mine will take a subservient position. You would be taking orders from doctors all your life. I want you to be in a position where you *give* orders! If you are interested in medicine, then I insist you take a full medical degree."

The mother paid no heed to her daughter's longing. She did not consider her daughter's genuine gifts and temperament. She waved aside the fact that her daughter did not *want* to give orders but did want to nurse people. My friend was dissuaded from her genuine guidance from God and subsequently entered a field that was not fulfilling for her, work that did not have her name on it.

> There are varieties of gifts, but the same Spirit; and there are varieties of services, but the same Lord; and there are varieties of activities, but it is the same God who activates all of them in everyone (1 Cor. 12:4-6).

In the same way, healthy spiritual direction does not prescribe one method of spiritual practice. We can respond to God in limitless ways. Introverts relate to God in a different way from extroverts. People who like structure approach daily prayer quite differently from those who need more spontaneity. Some choose to pray for an hour each morning; others throughout the day. God made our types of personality, loves us as we are, and reaches out to us through the genuine persons we are.

Certainly we often do unfold and change as we grow. Our deeply hidden or sleeping gifts and powers emerge in the most surprising ways, so we need to be open to possible inner changes. But that kind of evolving differs entirely from pushing or coercing inner changes according to our own or others' agendas and expectations.

For example, as a shy and introverted child and teenager, I was terrified of public speaking. The few times I was made to do it in high school were agonizing. No one was more surprised than I when in college I joined a loving, accepting student church group and began to discover newfound joy in public speaking. No one pushed me into it. No one told me it was God's will that I snap out of my fear. Occasionally and casually fellow students invited me to participate in worship leadership, but no one made me feel guilty if I said no. Eventually I began to volunteer. It was not easy, and I had setbacks. But I was allowed to find my own timing and learn from my mistakes. As my confidence grew, so did my joy. Speaking began to become not only more natural but even exciting. I learned to speak as I learned to swim in deep water, bit by bit, inch by inch into the depths. Then joy! That's how I learn.

God is gentle with our resistances. Resistances are not just obstacles to be broken down. We need to respect, look at, and listen to our resistances because we will learn a lot about ourselves, our fears, wounds, powers, and our sleeping gifts. Sometimes a resistance signifies a need for healing. Sometimes it represents a power we fear and a need for gentle encouragement. Sometimes resistance is a warning from God that a choice is wrong for us.

Our bodies also warn us if a fear needs healing or if a project is not right for us. If we experience strange body aches, rapid breathing, muscle tension, or new vulnerability to infection, we need not only to check these out medically but also consider the possibility that such symptoms may be warnings that our choices are causing us stress.

What if we don't notice resistances but just plunge enthusiastically into each new project, only later discovering we have made a mistake? Eager, generous people often act in the glow of the moment. How do we discern God's guidance if *everything* at first seems to have our name on it?

Or what if we have never really known our own "name" or asked ourselves what kind of person we really are? Usually this means we have come from families that never encouraged exploration of individual uniqueness and gifts. How do we discern God's guidance if we've always expected to do whatever we were supposed to do, as determined by others?

If we make mistakes either because everything seems to have our name on it or because we simply don't know our name— our real self—we need to reflect on our past experiences. Can we remember the characteristics of and the feelings surrounding choices that turned out to be mistaken? Were there warning signals? What were the results? Will we recognize the signals, the warnings, the characteristics, the inner feelings next time? Can we remember the surrounding feelings, advance signs, the characteristics of choices that turned out to be *right* for us? Will we recognize those signals the next time?

We noted earlier that just as God's sheep bonded to the shepherd, we will begin to be transformed into the nature of the Shepherd not by imitation but by transformation. In learning to recognize our personal name as called by God, we will focus increasingly on the unique personhood of individuals around us. We will begin to devote personal attention to those who need our help. We will listen to their stories, observe their characteristics, hear their genuine needs and longings. We will no longer generalize about people: "Women always . . ." "You know what men are like." "Teenagers are . . ." "Old people ought . . ." Each person will be unique in our eyes.

When asked for guidance we will try to help people listen to their own selves. We will encourage them to explore their particular needs, longings, wounds, gifts. We will support their discovery of what kind of persons they really are and tell them God loves those persons.

No longer will we say, "This always works for me; therefore, it ought to work for you." No longer will we push another by saying, "This is a worthy cause and you ought to get involved"; or, "This job needs doing and it is your duty to do it." Instead, we will try to help others to recognize their genuine gifts.

The prophet Isaiah had a vision of a healed, transformed world, a holy mountain in which all the different animals exult not only in their own uniqueness but equally in one another's uniqueness. This passion for one another's authentic being forms the basis of justice and harmony.

> The wolf shall live with the lamb,
>   the leopard shall lie down with the kid,
> . . . .
> The cow and the bear shall graze,
>   their young shall lie down together;
> They will not hurt or destroy
>   on all my holy mountain;
> for the earth will be full of the knowledge of the LORD
> as the waters cover the sea (Isa. 11:6, 7, 9).

The *knowledge* of God does not mean intellectual concepts. When the Bible speaks of knowledge, it means intimate, personal union. In other words, the more closely we are bonded with God, the more we are able not merely to tolerate differences and divergences but to welcome them joyously.

Jesus is saying the exact same thing in his shining story. His message radiates: The deeper the bond between Shepherd and sheep, the more meaningful is the personal name.

Reflection and Meditation

He determines the number of the stars; he gives to all of them their names.

—PSALM 147:4

Make yourself comfortable in a relaxed way. You can sit up, lie down, or take a quiet walk alone. Think of particular guidance you received either recently or long ago. Was it directed to you personally in your own specific situation? What were the results? Think of a choice you face now. What guidance are you receiving? From whom? How do you feel about it? Do you feel any inner resistance? Listen to your resistance. Where does it seem to come from? Does the resistance feel like a warning? Or does it feel like an old negative habit whose time for healing has come?

Does your heart lift with the guidance you are now receiving? Or do you experience a sense of heaviness? What is your body saying to you?

When you feel ready, relax your body and take a few slow, deep breaths, then breathe naturally. Think of God's love enfolding you. Think (or picture) the living Jesus near you, Jesus who cares deeply about you and your problem and who knows you as a unique person.

Express your problem and your feelings about it in your

own words. Now rest in silence for as long as you need, relaxed but alert and expectant. Does a special thought, a special feeling, an inner word, an inner symbol or picture, or a memory come to conscious awareness? Focus on what comes uppermost in your thought or feeling. Does it seem to apply to your present problem? In what way?

If nothing arises, don't push for anything. Know that God's love enfolds you and that God is speaking to you at a deep level even if you feel nothing. It may take more time for a special awareness to rise.

When ready, stretch; massage your face and hands lightly, and bring your meditation to a gentle close.

Set Free from Intrusion and Compulsion

Very truly, I tell you, anyone who does not enter the sheepfold by the gate but climbs in by another way is a thief and a bandit.

—JOHN 10:1

God's guidance never forces us. We are set free to choose. Pushing or coercion by another person, a community, a teaching, or a spiritual program in the area of our personal choices is not of Christ's Holy Spirit.

Forty-nine years ago I opened an eagerly awaited letter from my church superintendent. For years he had helped and encouraged me in my ministry, appointing me to interesting student pastorates and missions. These were unusual opportunities for a woman theological student at that time. I looked on him as a friend as well as a spiritual mentor and highly respected church leader.

I had written to him about my engagement and marriage plans with another theological student, expecting his interest and his good wishes. His letter was a great shock: "Your engagement is disappointing news. You have put your hand on the plow and are now looking back. You have turned away from God's call. A woman cannot be both minister and wife. She must choose. Under such circumstances, you should not be ordained. If I were on your ordination committee, I would have to vote against you."

Fortunately he was *not* on my ordination committee, which was in a different conference. It was even more fortunate that I recognized, almost at once, that this was not God's guidance but human *goading*. A rigid mind-set about what a woman minister should and should not do motivated this man's response.

I knew the superintendent was sincere, but many sincere people speak from inner programming, thinking it is God. As with many others, he was manipulating and twisting scripture to fit his own ideology and calling that interpretation God's will. In many ways the man had been a blessing in my life, but for all his sincerity and goodness, he could have seriously damaged my life. Had I followed his guidance, I would have sacrificed either a deep and genuine call to ministry or a marriage that for forty-nine years has blessed both me *and* my ministry.

This person did not enter the sheepfold by the valid gate. Though he had been friend to me, he was a potential thief of the life to which God called me.

Certainly we need to express our thoughts and concerns to others honestly. Certainly we need to express tough love in destructive situations, especially when guiding children or young persons endangering themselves and others. Certainly we need to set our own boundaries. But the guidance that comes through God's gate never rides roughshod over another's free will with pejorative judgments and manipulative threats, equating one's own opinion with the will of God.

In my family, when one of us would start pushing another (for the other's own good of course!), the response was, "You're not a loving shepherd. You've become a *shoving leopard*!" We laughed but also realized the damage even small trespasses can inflict on one another.

> Other people's definitions of us are not just absurd—if unchallenged, they erect prison walls around us. As they rise higher, the light of awareness fades. The world darkens. We lose freedom, safety, confidence, convictions, and sometimes ourselves.[1]

When Jesus said, "All who came before me are thieves and bandits," he obviously was not speaking of the prophets and spiritual leaders of earlier times. He honored the prophets. In the context of this passage, I see these words as a warning against those who barge in with their own plans, agendas, and expectations *before* God's fullness of time, before God's own answer unfolds, before the true Shepherd comes for us.

Sometimes a well-meaning friend appears early at the sheepfold gate before the true shepherd arrives. This friend means no harm and intends to do the shepherd a favor, bringing the sheep out to start them on the trail perhaps. But this well-intentioned trespasser does not know the true shepherd's plans. Perhaps the shepherd is arranging a different route that day to a new grazing area. Perhaps the shepherd has planned to postpone or cancel the day's outing because a storm is coming or because some of the sheep show signs of illness or are about to give birth. Meaning well, the trespasser actually is doing great harm.

I helped my mother plant a small vegetable garden when I was a child. Early one morning I planned a great surprise for her. Seizing a trowel, I set to work vigorously weeding for an hour. I was surprised at the number of new weeds that apparently had grown overnight. My mother was very gentle with me later as she surveyed the devastation. I had uprooted all the new young plants she had just put in the night before!

As a young minister, I made many presumptuous mistakes, convinced I knew best, rushing in to advise and guide others before God's purpose and plan had time to unfold and reveal themselves. I remember one especially tragic occasion. A young woman in my church was due to be married in less than a month. I had counseled these two fine young people; all the arrangements had been made for a lovely ceremony: music, dresses, flowers, reception. We had read and reflected together on the meaning of the words in the marriage service.

Then the young woman was diagnosed with a seriously disabling neurological disease. Her anguished fiancé came to talk with me. What should they do? What if she got worse? He loved her, but could he handle a chronic illness either emotionally or financially? I listened to him, or at least thought I was listening, but I was on the side of young love. I did not help him realistically pay attention to the grim prognosis or listen at depth to his worry. I knew what *I* would have decided and would have done in those circumstances. I encouraged him to go ahead with the marriage if she agreed. I told him possibly a happy marriage would help heal her or send the disease into remission.

I was mistaken. Within a year the wife was a helpless invalid and her husband deeply embittered. I look back in sorrow. I had not coerced him, but my enthusiasm was ignorant and presumptuous. I should have listened more closely to his reservations and urged him to wait—to think, pray, talk with others, and listen for God's answer to unfold.

"Thief" and "bandit." Are those names too strong for well-meaning trespassers? Not when we realize they are pushing themselves between us and God's answer. "Get behind me, Satan! You are a stumbling block to me," Jesus said to Peter, his close friend and the future rock of the church (Matt. 16:23) when Peter tried in his controlling way to stop Jesus from going to Jerusalem and facing death there. Personally, I have always believed Jesus did not say this with anger to Peter, and certainly not with a scornful shout. I believe Jesus spoke firmly but lovingly, perhaps with a smile as if to say, "There you go again! Pushing me around for my own good."

Jesus not only firmly maintained his own freedom of choice but also respected the free choice of others. When the rich young man turned sorrowfully away from the invitation to be Jesus' disciple, Jesus grieved because he had loved this man. But Jesus did not run after him pleading and pushing. He rebuked the disciples when they wanted to call down vengeful fire from heaven on the towns that did not welcome them. When Martha of Bethany asked Jesus to make her sister, Mary, come back into the kitchen and cook, Jesus defended Mary's decision to stay with him and talk. It is significant that though he preferred Mary's choice, he did not compel Martha to make the same decision.

How tragic that our churches through centuries have so often followed the pushing, controlling ways of Peter and

Martha, all in Jesus' name. The coercive minister I visited (chapter 3) told her members if they left the church, what remained of their lives would be full of disaster, degeneration, spiritual disintegration. For some of her victims this prediction became a self-fulfilling prophecy. Fearing her curse, those who did leave were haunted for years by nightmares, flashbacks, depression, guilt, severely damaged sense of self-worth, and a persistent distrust of organized religion or spiritual leadership. Some were afraid of the Bible, because she had so frequently quoted from it in a threatening, condemnatory way.

Such a travesty of spirituality is not merely well-meaning misguidance. It is a predatory destruction and devouring. Of those who mislead destructively Jesus said grimly, "The wolf snatches them and scatters them" (John 10:12).

I have met and talked with many victims of such spiritual predators. The "wolves" are found not only in the notorious cults but sometimes in mainline churches, counseling groups, professional training groups, ecclesiastical systems, political parties, as well as in families and workplaces. Predators have possessed and controlled whole nations as well as one-to-one relationships.

At first these predators do not seem destructive. Often they appear to express love, joy, and enthusiasm, presenting beautiful ideals of harmony and justice. Individuals who have hungered for such food are swept into relationship or commitment with these apparently gifted counselors or leaders. But fairly soon, the spiritual corrosion under the surface begins to manifest itself by coercion in small things, metastasizing into all areas of life, eating away at followers' freedom, vitality, spontaneity, and integrity. Eventually it becomes clear that independent thinking is discouraged; free choice is considered rebellion; pro-grammed response is required. The bottom line is total surren-der and submission to authority. That authority, whether individual leaders or group ethos, names itself God's will, God's guidance, spiritual maturing, the greater good, the higher vision; in these names the human spirit is violated.

Spiritual predators usually see themselves as righteous, prophetic figures. To resist them is to resist God or to resist the cause of righteousness. Often these abusers themselves have been victims of early abuse; they survive their pain by exerting power over others. Their sense of self-worth has been so dam-aged that they need to eat away at the integrity of others. Some, angry or frightened by the moral chaos and injustice in their environment or larger culture, force their own ideology as the only remedy, breaking the wills of all challengers and dissenters.

It is alarming to find these dynamics even in justice and reform movements. In a recent autobiography, a church leader reflected on his own active participation in aggressively vio-lent branches of the peace movements of the 1960s. He remembered the righteous anger that so quickly changed into fierce hatred. He spoke of the "arrogant virtue" assumed by leaders and participants intolerant of any view but their own, ready to use any violent means to bring about their vision.

Probably Jesus wrestled with the temptation to use fierce, arrogant coercion to bring about the kingdom of God there in the wilderness in the beginning of his ministry. The tempter offered all the manipulative shortcuts, as well as total, forcible control over the whole world. But Jesus knew that corruption on every level would be the result. He knew no one grows in emotional or spiritual maturity under coercion.

Chapter Five

Beware of false prophets, who come to you in sheep's clothing but inwardly are ravenous wolves. You will know them by their fruits (Matt. 7:15-16).

What are these fruits? How do we recognize the trespassers, the controllers, or the predators when they, perhaps quietly at first, invade our lives? We can ask ourselves these questions:

- Am I in any relationship, group, or system of guidance that makes me feel uneasy, anxious, dependent, powerless, unspontaneous?

- Are my questions heard or ignored? Am I allowed to disagree?

- Am I discouraged from seeking alternative viewpoints? Am I discouraged from maintaining friendships and ties with outsiders?

- If I do not comply with the guidance or expectations of others, is affection withheld? Am I punished, perhaps subtly, on some level?

- Do I feel more overall stress? Have I lost energy? Have my sleeping, eating, or exercise habits deteriorated since entering this relationship or following this guidance?

- Does the group, leader, or teaching consider my well-being and personal needs unimportant?

- What are my dreams telling me? Am I having unusual dreams of threat, fire, storms, earthquakes, tidal waves, bleeding wounds, break-ins? Does a certain theme keep repeating itself in my dreams?

- What is happening to other people in the same group or system of guidance? Does there seem to be a lot of sickness, depression, breakdowns, or addictive behavior?

- Are the leaders using coercive tactics that may seem in the early stages to be mild and harmless? (Chapter 10 offers additional discernment questions for communities.)

These symptoms suggest predatory intrusion and influence may be present, even if the group and its leaders are not aware of it. The guidance we're receiving may not be that of God's Holy Spirit. These signs warn of a creeping spiritual sickness.

We need to observe our own creeping coerciveness and intrusiveness. "Forgive us our trespasses," says the Lord's Prayer in the older translations. It is so painful to realize that we may have trespassed on another's life and violated someone's freedom and choices. We need to ask ourselves whether we really listen to others or push our own expectations and agendas on them. We need to observe how we respond bodily and emotionally when someone disagrees with us or resists our guidance. Does our body tense up? Do we recognize the signs of moving away from God's power toward the use of force? When we are guiding another person, we can say to ourselves: *Am I praying not that God will speak through me to the other but rather speak to us* both *as we share and discern together? I also need to learn and grow in God, and I have often been wrong.*

What a Lenten discipline this practice would be! What a *daily* discipline for growing together in the mind and nature of the Shepherd.

Chapter Five

Reflection and Meditation

For freedom Christ has set us free. Stand firm, therefore,
and do not submit again to a yoke of slavery.

—GALATIANS 5:1

You may wish to review some of the questions asked in this chapter, discerning whether you have been (or are now) intruded upon and whether you have come between another person and his or her free choice.

When ready, relax your body and rest for a while in the sureness of God's closeness. Take a few very slow, deep breaths, then breathe naturally.

If you have been coerced or spiritually abused by another (parent, teacher, spouse, pastor, or a system or ideology), think of Jesus Christ the healer and protector standing between you and the coercive influence or person. Sense the powerful protection around you. You might picture light, great wings, or God's arms or hands enfolding you. Or you may prefer to say inwardly, "I stand within the protection of the living Jesus Christ."

Ask the Christ to break the cords of bondage to this coercive person, group, or teaching; to draw its power out of your body, out of your personal space; to give this bondage over to God.

Ask that the powerful wind of God's Spirit may blow cleansing new air through you, or that God's cleansing river of light may flow through your whole body. You can either picture this or just ask for it in Jesus' name. Take a few deep breaths of the freedom that enfolds you. Then breathe naturally.

Sense Christ the protector standing between you and any coercive person or influence that may come your way in the future. Or simply pray: "In the name, and by the word of the living Jesus Christ, I am enfolded in the light of protection against anyone or anything who tries to trespass upon the freedom God has given me."

If you think you have coerced another person in his or her choices, ask God for forgiveness, and if possible ask forgiveness of that person as soon as possible. If you are no longer in touch with the person, inwardly ask that forgiveness. Pray after this manner (or in your own words): "In the name of Jesus Christ who sets us free, I set you, *[the person's name],* free from my expectations, my agendas. May your sense of freedom and strength be renewed. I will try never again to trespass upon your holy ground. May God continue to release us both."

When you feel ready, take a few deep, slow breaths; stretch; massage your face and hands gently; and bring your meditation to a close.

A Gate Opening Before Us

The gatekeeper opens the gate for him. . . . He . . . leads [his sheep] out.

—JOHN 10:3

*W*hen the true Shepherd guides us, a gate will open before us, leading to a wider place.

Early in my ministry I experienced a faith crisis. I was confused; I did not know where to turn. In those days, forty-five years ago, there were few, if any, special retreats for pastors. (We were not supposed to have faith crises!) Protestant pastors did not have spiritual directors. Most of us had never even heard of them. I prayed about my problem, but my doubts about prayer itself were part of the problem.

One day, quickly glancing through the book review section of the newspaper, I had a sudden, strong impulse to turn back to the previous page. There I found a short review that I had not noticed; it described the autobiography of a pastor whose life had been changed by his spiritual experiences. I sent for the book, and it changed my life. This book opened whole new vistas of spiritual realities. I wrote to the author, who promptly replied, suggesting other helpful books as well as prayer and healing groups I might explore. These books and contacts led me to new ways of praying and reading the Bible. They immeasurably deepened my Christian faith. They set my feet on a new path. They changed my ministry.

What (or who) prompted me to turn back that newspaper page? I had barely glanced at it and certainly had not seen that small item. Coincidence? I forget who said, "Perhaps coincidence. But I have noticed when I pray, coincidences happen. When I don't, *they* don't!"

Many people find their guidance in experiences like mine. They pray about a problem, place it in God's hands, and wait to see what happens, alert to changes that occur in the next few days. A significant phone call or a special letter will come. A life-changing book almost leaps into their hands. A new person enters their lives. A new project or job offer opens up. A conversation starts new lines of thought. They see an item in th newspaper. In short, what new realities appear? What gate opens?

God is a God of realities. When John the Baptist sent a message to Jesus asking if Jesus was really the Messiah, Jesus did not answer, "Yes, I am the Messiah because I say so." He pointed to the facts, the changed realities that were occurring:

> Go and tell John what you have seen and heard: the blind receive their sight, the lame walk, the lepers are cleansed, the deaf hear, the dead are raised, the poor have good news brought to them (Luke 7:22).

We do need the other guidelines as well, but increasingly I am paying special attention to what little or big changes occur in my daily life after I have prayed about a choice. Sometimes I take what I call a parable walk in silence, asking God to show me something important for me, a symbolic message from God. (Retreat participants find such walks meaningful.) Usually a small thing, such as a special flower or bush, the shape of a tree, a cloud, a rock, the activity of an ant or squirrel, catches my attention. It may be something I hear—the song of a bird, the wind in the trees, a distant bell or siren— or a fragrance or the texture of a leaf. But whatever comes to my attention, I imme-diately recognize it as the symbolic message. The sight, sound, or sensation may bring a memory to mind or evoke a new idea. It may be a sign of comfort and refreshment or a challenge. It is a message of significance for *me* at that moment in my life.

By no means is a message always solemn. Sometimes we can almost sense God's laughter. A few years ago I walked home feeling glum and downcast. I stumbled over a fist-sized stone in the gutter. Looking down at it, I instantly got the point, laughed, and brought it home. The little holes and scratches on the rock's surface had formed a face with a wide and cockeyed grin. A smiley-face formed by nature itself was a direct gift from God on that gloomy day. I have propped up the stone beside our tele-phone (the place where I am apt to take myself the most seriously), and I grin back at it when I walk by.

Other realities may change, such as dreams. Once I was struggling with the elusive focus for a book I was trying to write. One night I dreamed I was told to read certain verses in scrip-ture. When I woke up, I opened my Bible to those verses and found the central, integrating theme for the book.

Chapter Six

I have noticed that the genuine guidance dreams differ from ordinary dreams, which rise from the remnants of the day usually with a vague, scattered, nonsequential character. The guidance dream is clear, powerful, coherent, and often in color. Such dreams are personally significant and unforgettable.

We may find a change in the deep longings that rise within us. God often speaks through our longings—not every passing desire but the deep-rooted yearning of the heart. We may find a new longing surprising, even disconcerting.

"Why am I so fascinated with color recently?" an older woman confided in me. "I've always been the intellectual type— definitely left brain. When I go to the mall, I head for the bookstore. But now I'm pressing my nose against the clothing stores. I hang around cosmetic counters. I hunger for flower and garden shows. I'm changing my curtains and plan to repaint my rooms. I'm bored with beige and long for color. Am I becoming frivolous in my old age? Shouldn't I be thinking of holy things?"

But color *is* a holy thing. Jesus spoke lovingly of the splendor of flowers and the significance of festive garments at a wedding. The rainbow in scripture symbolizes God's fidelity. The book of Revelation describes the radiance of precious stones in the walls of the holy city. Perhaps my friend's newly awakened longing for color and beauty signaled a deep part of her nature was bursting through in holy need for God's revitalization of her body and spirit.

Are these new longings always holy guidance? Or might they be the beginning of an unhealthy addiction? Can we trust them?

We need to ask ourselves:

• Does this new interest harm me or anyone else?

- Does it cause me to neglect important responsibilities?
- Does it cause me to lie and deceive?
- Am I losing interest in everyday life and my relationships?
- Does it lessen my concern for others?

Affirmative answers to any of those questions would be warning signs. Compulsive addictions, whether relationships, projects, hobbies, even certain forms of spiritualities, narrow us, constrict us, and close down our healthy interest and response to the life and people around us.

I stepped into a gambling casino once to make a phone call. The flashing strobe lights and the harsh music didn't horrify me nearly as much as the fixed, intense gaze on the faces of people working the machines. Like sleepwalkers, most of them were closed off, deaf to any other interest, any other person. The casino had no windows. Customers could not see the sky, the trees, the clouds, or any natural light. They were narrowed down to one thing, the money machine in front of them. I still carry this inner picture, symbolic of all our addictive prisons of the spirit, which are *any* fixations that close us off to God's world around us.

Blockages to God can include worthy and righteous activities! Overwhelming, passionate convictions or flaming zeal for a cause may constitute part of a genuine call from God. All the great reformers of the world were intensely involved with their transforming work. We may feel that we're engaged in something we *must* do, no matter the cost! But even in the grip of powerful conviction, we still need to look at the realities, responsibilities, and relationships of our lives and ask:

- Do my convictions lead me to act intrusively and coercively with others, brushing aside their valid needs and their free choices?

- Do my convictions lead me to arrogant virtues that scorn the thoughts and viewpoints of others?

- Do my convictions lead me to abandon my ordinary responsibilities and commitments? It is usually a sign of predatory misguidance if we are urged or forced to abandon family, friends, daily work, and self-care in the name of ideology or spirituality.

A formerly prevalent attitude toward church work exemplifies how deep conviction may misguide us. For centuries up until recent times, pastors, missionaries, spiritual leaders, and their families were urged to put in second place family life, health, and private time for renewal. All that mattered was service to God, which was equated with service in the church. A dreadful toll in ruined health, dysfunctional or even abusive family life, breakdowns, and addictive behavior resulted.

In recent decades a healthy change of attitude has prevailed in many churches. Increasingly, pastors and other full-time Christian workers hear that their marriage vows to love and cherish their partners are as holy as their ordination vows. Health, recreational renewal, private time, and emotional healing are no longer considered selfish luxuries but vital aspects of Christian witness and wholeness in Christ. When joined to Christ, *all* that we are and do is an aspect of our Christian witness, not just the church work part.

At times in Christian life and history, communal evil is so deep that we must risk our ordinary responsibilities in order to witness to God's truth. But there is a vast difference between such extraordinary sacrifice and *neglect* of our commitments on a daily basis as if they were of little value.

But what about the disciples? Did they not leave everything to follow Jesus? Yes, some were invited to do so, but not everyone who loved and followed Jesus was asked to become a traveling disciple. He chose the ones who had special gifts for that life and who apparently were free enough to undertake such a life. Jesus sent others home to witness to their neighbors what God had done for them. His close friends, Mary, Martha, and Lazarus of Bethany, did not join him on the road. They kept their home and daily life in Bethany and provided Jesus a sheltering home when he needed rest and refreshment.

If we have given our whole heart to God and God's guidance and God's way of love, we have already become "a living sacrifice, holy and acceptable to God" (Rom. 12:1) in every small or great thing we do, whether in the home or out in the world. The ways of living this holy life are wide and varied.

Sometimes the opened gate does mean a different job, a different way of life, a different set of responsibilities and relationships. But at other times the opened gate may lead to a different way of doing our usual work, a new way of responding to others, an alternative way of praying, a transformed attitude toward ourselves, a different way of relating to God.

In any case, though, there will be a difference in our lives. A gate will open.

Chapter Six

Reflection and Meditation

Ask and it will be given you; search, and you will find; knock, and the door will be opened for you.

—MATTHEW 7:7

Sit or lie down in comfort. Or take a slow, solitary walk. Think about a problem or choice you have been facing. Have you prayed about it? If so, has anything notable happened subsequently? Have you received a special letter, a book, a phone call? Had a significant conversation? Has a new dream come to you? Do you feel a new deep longing? Has something ended?

Does this new event relate to your problem? Tell God again about your problem, clearly and to the point in your own words. (Of course, God already knows all about it. It is we who need to clarify in our minds just what we need.)

You might wish to picture or just think of Jesus sitting next to you as a special friend. It is not necessary to picture him in a long white robe. Let him be near you in whatever way you need right now. Talk about the problem or write it down as if you were writing a letter to Jesus.

Or think of a picture, object, or symbol that expresses the problem and give it to Jesus. You could put the letter or object under a cross, behind a religious picture, in the leaves or blossoms of a potted plant, or in some other private place that makes you think of God's enfolding love.

If you are walking, gaze around with openness but without trying to make something special happen. Does anything especially draw your attention: a bird, a tree, a cloud, a rock, a pinecone, a house, a person passing by, a fragrance, or a sound? If so, is this a symbol for you? Does it bring a particular memory to mind? a new idea? refreshment or comfort? What is God saying through this object, sound, fragrance, or touch?

Or simply pray (using your own words, of course): "Loving guide, my true Shepherd, I give my problem to your hand and heart. Show me the open gate. I know you hear me and that a way is opening for me. I give you thanks."

Bring your meditation to a gentle close. In the next few days be alert and aware of any significant change, whether small or large, in your life.

CHAPTER SEVEN

Green Pastures of Our Hearts

Whoever enters by me will . . . come in and go out and find pasture.

—JOHN 10:9

I came that they may have life, and have it abundantly.

—JOHN 10:10

*T*errified, I preached my first sermon in a tiny rural church during a Michigan blizzard. I was eighteen and a member of a church college group that occasionally would send out teams of three or four to lead services and preach in small churches without full-time pastors.

It had begun to snow at dawn, and I was the only member of the team who lived close enough to reach the church. I was still nervous about the public speaking, but I had agreed to prepare a five-minute homily if one of the other members actually gave the sermon. I struggled through the door; with the wind whipping around me, I saw the little congregation staring at me expectantly, and now I realized it was up to me to lead a whole service and preach a whole sermon, for the first time in my life!

By the time I gave my sermon title I was in such a muddle of emotion, I probably was not aware of the incongruity: The storm wind howled and shook the little building; the lights flickered; the handful of worshipers wondered if they would be able to get home at all, while a frightened young woman up front announced her sermon in a trembling voice: "The Joy of Being a Christian"!

Strangely, the joy actually *was* there, running through my nervousness, my awkwardness, the storm outside, like a deep, sparkling river. This joy comes at the strangest times, in the most unexpected situations. Why are we surprised? Jesus promised us joy, the inner pastures, life abundant.

But what about sacrifice, self-denial, the way of the cross? Do we inappropriately deny these Christian priorities if we speak of joy? Is there an innate contradiction here? Jesus knew all about the risks of the life of love. He knew about the valleys of the shadow and the predatory enemies. The beloved Twenty-Third Psalm is realistic. "The road is hard that leads to life," Jesus had told his friends (Matt. 7:14). Nevertheless, the guided life also offers abundant pasture, even in the midst of peril, pain, and predators.

Being guided by God does not guarantee we will have perfect families, perfect jobs, perfect health, with no problems or challenges. But genuine guidance *does* mean we will experience basic fulfillment and renewal. It means we will feel vitally alive in our giving and receiving. It means that our lives will not be barren but fruitful. We will not be left empty, desolate, depleted. Abundance will be present at our center.

The word *abundance* means an overflowing fullness. The root of the word is associated with undulation, a rhythmic, wavelike motion, like the flow of tides in an ocean. When we walk in God's guidance, a full, rhythmic flow of life pulses within us.

If we are living our choices without this sense of renewal and fulfillment, something is wrong, even if outwardly this life appears good and righteous. We may have made a choice that is not right for us. Perhaps we are living our choice in an unguided way. Or we may be under the guidance of someone or something that is not the true Shepherd.

Of course, all of us will experience occasional times of frustration, uneasiness, lowered vitality. Jesus knew what it was to feel tired and lonely. He sometimes cried, became angry just as we do. But if inner storms persist and become the norm in our life, they are warning signs.

Exceptions, of course, are such conditions as clinical depression or severe hormonal imbalance. Such genuine bodily illnesses profoundly affect one's sense of well-being. They are not signs of spiritual malaise or misguidance. Instead, these conditions signal the need for bodily healing and should not make us feel ashamed or unworthy. When working through these conditions, we will, for a while, need to depend more on the other guidelines rather than the sense of joy and fulfillment for spiritual discernment. It is also important to know that God works with us for our healing, reaching us through medical practitioners as well as through prayer. God is always on the side of healing.

But if we are not challenged by such physical conditions, a prolonged absence of fulfillment and inner joy tells us to look carefully and prayerfully at our recent choices. I once took a church job that involved hours of organizing, networking, contacting strangers, and making surveys. It was an interesting, worthwhile job—for someone else. For me, it became draining and exhausting. I dreaded getting up in the morning. I actually did the work fairly competently, but it was joyless. Fortunately the job was temporary; had it continued for years, I think I would have become ill.

This job experience contrasted sharply with others I have had. One year, for example, I was secretary in a hospital operating room. The pay was abysmal; the work was hard and intensive; and I made many mistakes. But I felt alive and fascinated with what I was doing. During my years as adjunct faculty member at a theological seminary, I felt the same way. I wanted to *run*, not walk, to my classes, though again the pay was low and the work demanding. Obviously I enjoyed some aspects of the work less than others, but those twelve years of teaching vitally involved and fulfilled my deep self.

Where *do* sacrifice and self-denial come in then? If we study Jesus' teaching on self-denial, we learn that we are *not* asked to deny ourselves because suffering is good for us or because God considers happiness unimportant. It is the other way around. *Because* God wants us to experience deep joy and fulfillment, we are challenged to give up lesser desires that may block the great central joy.

For example, Jesus told a story of a farmer who found a box of treasure when plowing in a field: "then *in his joy* he goes and sells all that he has and buys that field" (Matt. 13:44-46, italics added). He sacrificed all that he had formerly owned and valued, but now his great joy swallowed up his loss.

A wedding service provides another example of lesser joys surrendered to the greater joy. What is *really* going on at that flower-decked altar? What is *really* happening amid all the music, candlelight, laughter, and celebration? It is sacrifice and self-denial at their profoundest! Up there two adult people are giving their lives away, promising to forsake all others, vowing to cherish and care for another person for life in spite of any sickness, poverty, hardship. Think of all that each is giving up. No more dates with old boy- and girlfriends, no more spur-of-the-moment decisions, no more putting one's own amusements and tastes first. No more being responsible only to oneself. It is a genuine dying to one's old life and self happening at that altar, an incredible sacrifice! But no one uses these words at a wedding. No one is thinking in these terms—least of all the sacrificial "victims"! The old life is swallowed up in the joy of a deeper love, a reborn life.

Count the number of times Jesus uses the word *joy* at the Last Supper in John's Gospel, on that dark night when he is betrayed. Those words reflect the way he genuinely felt about his life, even in the midst of grief, loss, and pain.

Somehow in our Christian teaching through the centuries we got the concept of sacrifice twisted around. We taught that suffering was sent by God because it was good for us. We taught that the more we suffered, the more worthy we were of God's love. A cult of suffering and sacrifice for its own sake developed in some forms of theology and spirituality.

Christians had forgotten Jesus' teaching that sacrifice is only to clear the way, to make space for greater, deeper joys.

Christians forgot that when Jesus spoke of joy and abundant life, he meant just that.

But what about the cross we are invited to share? Isn't that by definition an invitation to a life of pain and sacrifice? The cross Jesus invites us to share is not the same as illness, accident, or an unhappy life. Our cross is our free choice to lift the burden of suffering from another person. We can recognize our own cross by special signs, in many ways similar to the general signs of guidance.

- We are set free to choose our cross or refuse it.

- We will feel a deep, authentic calling to our cross.

- Though the pain and sacrifice are real, we also will experience a definite joy, strength, and renewal at our center, even though sometimes they grow dim temporarily.

- Our ability to love will deepen.

- We will observe signs of fruitfulness, some positive results and response, at least at times. (Consistent lack of any positive results, consistent frustration, and blocks may indicate we have picked up the wrong cross.)

- An "angel" will be sent to comfort and strengthen us, even as one was sent to Jesus in Gethsemane. The angel usually comes in unexpected ways: a person, a book, an experience of beauty, a lifting of the heart, and so on. But it always brings comfort. Who or what have been your angels when you needed them?

- A "Simon of Cyrene" will also be sent to help us lift our cross, our commitment, our chosen task of love, in very practical ways, even as Simon carried the cross beam for

Jesus. Our Simons also come in many different ways with definite and solid assistance. It is helpful to recollect our past Simons.

If these signs are not present, we may have taken a cross— committed ourselves to a task—that was meant for someone else. Why do we make such mistakes? At times of decision, all other signs of guidance seem to be present; only later do we realize that no joy, no pastures—either outer or inner—abide in our choice.

A young minister accepted a call to a church that welcomed him warmly. The work seemed at first to suit his special gifts, and all plans fell quickly into place. He was ready and eager, but within a few months he felt profoundly stressed. His health deteriorated, and the joy had gone out of his ministry.

What went wrong? In his case, no one had told this young minister, nor had he asked, about the history of the church that called him. He did not know about its deep communal wounds and traumas. He did not know about the small abusive clique within the church that domineered the passive members. He had not heard that several recent ministers had broken down or become ill. In other words, his choice could not be considered truly a free one, because it was based on ignorance of the facts. Had the minister looked into the background of the congrega- tion, he could have made an informed choice, discerning whether he had the special gifts and stamina needed for healing work in a hurt and hurtful community.

Sometimes we brush past early warning signs in our enthu- siasms. They seem so slight we ignore them. Certainly there are no absolutely risk-free relationships. If we expect that, we will live in a state of emotional paralysis. God calls us to adventure, not into lockups of caution. Nevertheless, there are usually some indications if we are undertaking an adventure that is not right for us.

For example, I have known several disintegrating marriages in which one spouse had protested ahead of time that he or she was not ready for a marriage commitment. Usually such protests should be heard and taken seriously, for these individuals are speaking the simple truth.

Often in our eagerness to be helpful, and hoping to live up to the expectations of others, we may commit ourselves to a task before considering whether it is appropriate for the type of person we really are. I made that mistake when I agreed to the church job described earlier in this chapter. Taking on a commitment because we think if *we* don't do it, nobody will, is as misguided as saying, "If *I* don't marry this person, *nobody* will!"

Sometimes we make a good choice, but old unhealed inner wounds of fear, shame, or anger block us. Our wound would become a block to us whatever choice we made. In such a case, a different commitment would not release the block; we need deep healing before we can move forward with any commitment. "You anoint my head with oil" (Ps. 23:5) refers to the healing ointment given the sheep even in the green pastures. Our old wounds of memory, abuse, trauma, injustice, emotional deprivation—if not healed—have the power to pour toxicity into our present life and relationships.

Rigid habits of emotional response and narrow, judgmental thinking that may come down to us through many generations can have the same effect. These prisons of the spirit (which we may not even realize enclose us) are major causes of joylessness, major blocks to inner abundance, even in righteous lives.

Sometimes joylessness results not from wrong choices but from deep fatigue of body and spirit. Many who flatter themselves that they are experiencing a "dark night of the soul" are actually just drained and exhausted people. Deep fatigue does not always manifest itself as obvious tiredness. *Hyper*activity, dulled emotional response, irritability, inability to concentrate, chronic restlessness, or anxiety may indicate serious fatigue. (I have learned that I will begin to feel inappropriately anxious when I am very tired without realizing it.)

We need to check out the possibility of depression of course, but also we need to ask ourselves if we have ignored or neglected the *outer* pastures of our lives. Do we schedule intentional times of rest and enjoyment? Does our prayer time allow for quiet reflection and listening to what God is saying to us in our deep selves? Do we listen to what our bodies (our spiritual guides and partners) are trying to tell us about our stressful habits? Do we claim for ourselves little "sabbaths" through the day, letting our five senses feed us through sight, hearing, taste, touch, fragrance? The deep, sparkling river of inner joy is also fed by the little streams of outer joys—rest, play, and sensory nourishment.

Sometimes joylessness arises from the choices of *others*. God has given us all the dangerous gift of free will; without it, we could not grow into full human beings actively sharing in God's love and creativity. Other people, acting out of their unhealed wounds or the misuse of their free will, may make choices that wound our spirits; they may become stumbling blocks for us; or they may drain us of hope and vitality.

Chapter Seven

If a relationship or commitment is turning our light into darkness and destroying our joy, hope, and health, God may be calling us *out* of this destructive commitment. Emotional and spiritual destruction is not the same as a true cross. Our true crosses, though painful, renew our strength and faith; they never destroy our spirit. When God calls us out of a relationship that fosters inner disintegration and death, it is a holy call of guidance. Jesus received such a call to leave his hometown, Nazareth, when its citizens tried to destroy him. It was not the right time, place, or the right cross. He *chose* his time and place not as a victim but in redemptive freedom, speaking of joy as well as sorrow.

Whatever the cause of our joylessness, it points to a need for deep change on some level, for God does not will joylessness for us. Bringing abundance to people mattered to Jesus. He fed the five thousand not with a beverage and a small bag of pretzels, but, as we are told, "All ate and were filled; and they took up twelve baskets of broken pieces" (Mark 6:42-43). He fed them abundantly not just with food but also with hope, comfort, healing, renewal, challenge, and joy.

I see a new paradigm, a different model, for our liturgies and worship services within the great twenty-first chapter of John's Gospel. In this account of Jesus' resurrection appearance on the shores of the lake one early morning, Jesus calls in, welcomes, warms, feeds, and heals his disciples—body and spirit—*before* any discussion about Peter's denial. This model challenges our liturgical custom of putting confession of sin so near the beginning of our worship. This customary placement is based on theologies and spiritualities of innate shame and guilt. It is based on the belief (shared by many ancient pagan religions) that we have to be *cleansed* before we can approach God. But the God we see through Jesus is the lover of our souls. Jesus never demanded confession and cleansing before he helped and healed those who came to him. Sometimes he would tell them their sins were forgiven, but usually there was no mention of their sin at all.

Confession has a vital place in any relationship of honest love. We do need to work through the hurts, denials, and wounds of trust if love is to grow. But let us look at how Jesus did it. He built the fire and cooked breakfast for the disciples. Then he stood by the water's edge and called the disciples to shore. They came, bringing with them the fish he had guided them to find. He invited them to sit by the fire where they could warm themselves, and he fed them. Only *after* they were warmed and fed did he turn to Peter and lead him through the confession and healing with great gentleness.

Interwoven with Peter's commitment to love is Jesus' empowering commission: "Feed my lambs. . . . Tend my sheep. . . . Feed my sheep." The strength to feed others rises from the tenderness of the warmth, nourishment, and comfort that has been given.

What new, empowering forms of liturgy and worship might rise from the healing, transforming encounter between Jesus and his friends? Comfort and feed God's people *before* confession. It occurred to me in church one day that the Lord's Prayer also gives priority to feeding: "Give us this day our daily bread" comes before "Forgive us our trespasses [debts or sins]."

Abundant joy and sacrificial love were never intended to be opposites or even separate. They flow together as the great river of God's grace. They are simultaneous. They are one.

Reflection and Meditation

I will open rivers on the bare heights,
and fountains in the midst of the valleys.

—ISAIAH 41:18

Your builders outdo your destroyers.

—ISAIAH 49:17

Rest comfortably or take a quiet walk. Let your breathing flow fully and slowly through your body. Breathe naturally. God's love enfolds and flows through you. When you feel ready, slowly consider these questions:

- How do I really feel about my life and my choices?
- Is there underlying joy and sense of fulfillment?
- What are fruitful results in my life, my work, my relationships?
- Am I taking time for regular rest, fun, enjoyable things, making spaces for prayer and quietness?
- When I pray, do I take time to *listen* to what God is saying to me?
- What does my body feel right now? Do any areas feel tight, strained, tired? What is my body telling me about my choices, about my life?

Breathe again slowly and deeply, then naturally.

Think of an image or feeling that represents abundant renewal and joy. Might it be a spring of clear water flowing in fullness up from the ground? Kneel by the water or step into its current. Bathe your face and hands; drink from your hands. There is always enough. There is always more.

Or you might want to think of lying on the sand by the

ocean. The sand is warm. The gentle waves flow in and out, washing your whole body in a rhythmic, pulsing motion. There is always enough. There is always more. "You shall see and be radiant . . . because the abundance of the sea shall be brought to you" (Isa. 60:5). God brings fullness to you in this same over-flowing manner.

This may be enough for now. But if you feel ready, ask God to show in what ways you may be guided to new choices, new ways of living your choices, new ways of being healed, or new ways of claiming pasture in daily life.

Don't push anything. God hears you now, has always heard you, and even now God's response enfolds you though you may not yet see or feel it. Be calmly alert in the next few days for new guiding signs.

> I pray that you may have the power to comprehend, with all the saints, what is the breadth and length and height and depth, and to know the love of Christ that surpasses knowledge, so that you may be filled with all the fullness of God (Eph. 3:18-19).

Bring your meditation to a close with gentle stretching, light massage of face and hands. God enfolds you still as you go to your next experience.

CHAPTER EIGHT

Love More Inclusive

~

I have other sheep that do not belong to this fold. I must bring them also, and they will listen to my voice. So there will be one flock, one shepherd

—JOHN 10:16

I wonder how my life would have unfolded differently if a couple of students in our college church group had not noticed how solitary I was. My shyness was so acute that I would slip out the church's side door rather than have to talk to people at the front entrance. It never occurred to me to go to that young adult group on Sunday evenings. I had three or four friends, but I was not comfortable in groups. I was sure I would not know what to do or say. I would never fit in. I was an outsider.

Those two students joined me one Sunday at the side door, smiling warmly, and invited me to help fix the supper for the evening gathering. They asked if I would be willing to turn the pages of the hymnbook as one played the piano. This did not sound too scary, so I agreed, came that night . . . and the next

Sunday . . . and the next—entering the most transforming period of my life.

When we are guided by Jesus' Spirit, our love not only grows deeper, it grows more inclusive. It reaches out to embrace the outsider, to welcome the outcast, as those two students reached out and welcomed me.

Those two young people were not trying to enlarge the group, which more than a hundred college students regularly attended. They were not trying to compel me to conform to a special formula of creed and faith; though deeply centered around Jesus Christ, the group was tolerant of diverging inter-pretations of the faith. They cared that I was alone. They wanted to include me in a warm circle of love. A beautiful line in Psalm 68, which I prefer in the King James translation, says, "God set-teth the solitary in families" (Ps. 68:6).

Jesus' words about the sheep outside the fold have been mis-interpreted. They are not a mandate to compel people to enter a specific church, adhere to a specific theology, or conform to one standard of behavior. Such an interpretation only builds higher, thicker walls of exclusion. Jesus never compelled or excluded anyone. He longed to release us all from prisons of the spirit, not to build more prisons.

I believe Jesus was thinking of a shepherd who looks beyond the safety and security of his own well-cared-for flock. He scans the distant hills and the dry desert patches. He notices the lone sheep. He sees the homeless, wandering ones: perhaps baby sheep whose mothers had died or been taken by wild animals, wounded or sick sheep, sheep that were old and limping, preg-nant sheep. If these untended sheep were not already in pitiable condition, they soon would be, dying of hunger or sickness or vulnerable to wolves and mountain lions. Some shepherds would not even notice the homeless ones or would avoid them. An outsider always poses a risk to a clean, well-cared-for flock. But this shepherd is of God, whose love makes room for all, with no exclusions.

"One flock, one shepherd" means the heart of God that welcomes all. It is the work of Jesus' church to welcome all into that heart, making no distinctions, witnessing that in God's heart there are no outsiders, no outcasts.

Any so-called guidance that builds dividing walls is not God's guidance. The prophet Isaiah, whom Jesus loved and quoted, had made this clear hundreds of years earlier:

> Do not let the foreigner joined to the LORD say,
>> "The LORD will surely separate me from his
>>> people";
> and do not let the eunuch say,
>> "I am just a dry tree."
> . . . .
> for my house shall be called a house of prayer
>> for all peoples.
> Thus says the Lord GOD,
>> who gathers the outcasts (Isa. 56:3, 7, 8).

Such words were a shock; nothing was less acceptable than a foreigner unless it were a eunuch. No matter how righteous eunuchs might be personally, such people were considered a contamination. They were not allowed to enter sanctified places. No one should eat with them or enter their houses.

Jesus' actions were even more radical than Isaiah's words. Rather than remove walls, he acted as if those walls did not even exist! He welcomed the touch of a bleeding woman who sought

healing, though flowing blood was considered a serious contamination. He welcomed the presence and touch of a woman
of bad reputation who washed his feet. He talked with a Roman
soldier, praised his faith, and was prepared to set forth to the
Roman's house to heal his servant. He said not a word about the
fact that the Roman was a foreigner from a hated country. He
did not even try to convert him! He shared food with those who
collected taxes (they were considered despicable). He mingled
with and healed those ill with leprosy who were by definition so
unclean and outcast they were not allowed to enter the city.

Jesus visited foreign villages and healed the sick. He went
among the Samaritans who were considered not only impure
but heretical. He actually talked *alone* with a *woman*, who was a
Samaritan with a *bad reputation*, about *spirituality* (an
appalling act for a holy man on all five counts!) without trying
to convert her to orthodoxy but opening her troubled life for
closeness to God.

Jesus' disciples carried the same shattering, radical release to
other nations, other peoples who all had their own rigid laws of
exclusion. Paul described this new life of total welcome:

> There is no longer Jew or Greek, there is no longer slave
> or free, there is no longer male and female; for all of
> you are one in Christ Jesus (Gal. 3:28).

This wide welcome does not imply there are no distinctive
identities or enriching differences. Paul makes that clear in 1
Corinthians 12 when he talks about all the different, though
equally needed and valued, bodily parts, all with distinct
appearance and function but all part of the body harmony.

What does welcoming inclusiveness mean for us today?

Who are the foreigners, the eunuchs, the lepers, the tax collectors, the Samaritans among us now, whether in our personal or communal lives?

Even today some Christian communities build walls of exclusion. Some forbid women from serving as pastors or offering the sacraments simply *because* they are women. Some Christian communities forbid Christians who are not members of their particular church to share in the Eucharist. How can such exclusions be made in the name of Jesus who never put women in an excluded category, who shared the bread and wine of the Last Supper with Judas who would betray him, with Peter who would deny him, and with all the disciples, most of whom fled from him later that night? Some churches publish lists of suspect books whose authors—though Christ-centered—do not adhere to rigidly prescribed orthodoxy. In a recently publicized incident, a church expelled a little girl from Sunday school because her mother earned a meager living as a bar dancer.

Once I was informed by several members of a large retreat group in a mainline church that I was releasing demonic influence into the group. Why? Because I sometimes referred to scripture without instantly quoting chapter and verse and also because I challenged some of the condemnatory passages in the Old Testament. But didn't Jesus do both these things? No matter, I was letting in evil spirits! More than once I have been told I was not a Christian because I did not fit into rigidly defined limits.

How quickly we build up dividing walls again, as fast as God liberates us from these spiritual prisons. But did not Jesus say, "Enter through the narrow gate" (Matt. 7:13)? This sounds at first like new constrictions. But in the context of the Sermon on the Mount, and in the context of his whole spirit of giving freedom and release, the statement does *not* mean narrowness of love, rigidity of outlook. I believe Jesus was talking about clear centeredness, the unified focus of loving God with heart, soul, mind, and strength and our neighbor as ourselves. He was talking about our supreme, central priority of life, the supreme, central relationship with Christ, the living vine from which flows our joy and strength.

This unified central focus is to be clear, but it does not include judgment of others. Note that the passage in Matthew's Gospel about the narrow gate *opens* with these words: "Do not judge. . . . Why do you see the speck in your neighbor's eye, but do not notice the log in your own eye?" (Matt. 7:1, 3).

The central priorities in our own lives do not wall us off from interest in and conversation with others, even though we may not agree with them. Open responsiveness to others is one of the shining aspects of inclusive love.

Does this inclusiveness imply there are to be no rules of membership and leadership? I see two major criteria for communal welcome in Jesus' teaching: first, we are all to serve one another, not as slaves but as lover serves beloved. Secondly, no abuse is to be permitted on any level, whether hurtful acts, scorn, belittling, exploitation, arrogance, cover-ups, shaming, or any spiritual and emotional compulsion.

Ezekiel's powerful words convey a frightening picture of abuse based on the shepherd-and-sheep metaphor. This abuse can refer to home and family, church, workplace, politics, or government:

> As for you, my flock, thus says the Lord GOD: I shall
> judge between sheep and sheep. . . . Is it not enough for
> you to feed on the good pasture, but you must tread
> down with your feet the rest of your pasture? . . .
>
> I myself will judge between the fat sheep and the
> lean sheep. Because you pushed with flank and shoul-
> der, and butted at all the weak animals with your horns
> until you scattered them far and wide, I will save my
> flock, and they shall no longer be ravaged (Ezek. 34:17-
> 18, 20-22).

But what about those members who *do* push, hurt, and rav-
age? Are they not to be excluded? Certainly they must be
stopped. Submitting to abuse not only endangers the victim but
also endangers the emotional and spiritual health of the abuser.
There are churches, for example, where an individual or small
group will spearhead a vicious, destructive campaign against
the minister out of jealousy, need for power, fear and hatred of
anything nontraditional, or out of a doctrinal witch hunt. I have
seen several ministries destroyed this way and churches torn
apart. If such abuse is not stopped, the diseased arrogance grows
like a cancer.

Whether in a family situation or a in larger community,
separating the abuser may be necessary; at least firm borders
and limits need to be set. God does not require us to submit
to abuse. The provocative eighteenth chapter of Matthew's
Gospel discusses these issues with great realism. But even when
tough limits are set or separation is imposed, we are to witness
to the fact that no one is cast out of God's heart. God the
Shepherd forever loves and seeks all of us, even the abusers
among us. Preceding the passages in Matthew about the

possibility of separation we read the significant words below. Undoubtedly this passage refers to the abuser as well as to the victim of abuse.

> If a shepherd has a hundred sheep, and one of them has gone astray, does he not leave the ninety-nine on the mountains and go in search of the one that went astray? (Matt. 18:12)

Sometimes we may not consciously exclude others. Rather, we simply do not see them. We step over them as if they do not exist. Perhaps this behavior represents the ultimate abuse, the deepest lovelessness: not even to notice. Who are the ones in our personal lives, our homes, our neighborhoods, our wider communities, whose deep needs and silent cries we do not see or hear? Are our choices intensifying this nonawareness? If so, these choices are not guided by God.

What about our neglect of the living body of our own earth, which daily feeds and sustains us? What about cruelty to animals held in tight pens so they may grow fatter? What about the dangerous and stupid exploitation and pollution of earth, air, water? Ezekiel's vision speaks to us now as we consider how we abuse our environment every day out of ignorance and neglect:

> Is it not enough for you to feed on the good pasture, but you must tread down with your feet the rest of your pasture? When you drink of clear water, must you foul the rest with your feet? And must my sheep eat what you have trodden with your feet, and drink what you have fouled with your feet? (Ezek. 34:18-19)

Often we ignore or brush past someone's crying need because our minds are on "higher things." Many communities and teachings communicate only in generalities and categories. Individual persons are minimized for the sake of the "greater good." These practices exclude and dehumanize on a subtler but dangerous level.

I am moved by Jesus' encounter with the blind Bartimaeus who called frantically from the roadside. Jesus has every reason to ignore this man's cry. He is on his way for the last time to Jerusalem. He has just explained to his disciples what will happen to him there. He has intervened in a quarrel among them about who is to be foremost in his kingdom and explained to them *again* the true nature of leadership and greatness. How exasperating and depressing it must have been for Jesus to realize how fundamentally the disciples still misunderstand him.

A large, noisy crowd surrounds Jesus; everyone is trying to get his attention. Then an insignificant beggar by the roadside calls out to him in anguished need. "Many sternly ordered him to be quiet, but he cried out even more loudly. . . . Jesus stood still and said, 'Call him here'" (Mark 10:48-49).

Jesus stands still. He hears the cry; he focuses his full attention on Bartimaeus. He looks at him fully, as if Bartimaeus were the only person in the world at that moment. He is not thinking, *What does this one cry count when I see the crying need of the whole world?* He is not thinking, *I've got to get on to Jerusalem. Something much more important needs to be done there.* Bartimaeus matters.

As Jesus goes to the cross, he is in desperate pain and needs to focus on what awaits him, yet he hears and cares about the weeping women by the side of the road. They matter.

On the cross itself Jesus turns his full attention to the need of the thief suffering beside him. He looks fully into the eyes of his mother and the beloved disciple and makes a practical plan for his mother's care. For him, never is the individual person lost in a greater purpose.

I remember an event from over fifty years ago when I worked as secretary in the operating room of a large hospital. One of the surgeons was leaving the ward, exhausted after several hours of complicated surgery, probably reviewing not only the operations of that day but those of the next day. As he came down the hall, I noticed a tired cleaning woman walking just ahead of him. She suddenly tripped and dropped several towels from her overloaded cart. This surgeon, world-famous in his field, immediately stopped, picked up the towels, handed them to the woman with a warm smile, and then continued on his way.

I never forgot that incident. I see every detail as clearly as I did in 1953. It has become an almost sacramental parable for me. How that surgeon would laugh if he could read my solemn words about the exchange. It was a simple, natural thing for him. But in that event I saw God who never ignores any of us within the vast purposes of creation. Such an incident *is* the vast purpose of creation!

Are we inclusive toward ourselves? Do we pay attention to our own inner cries, hurts, and hungers? Loving and taking care of ourselves is not at all the same as selfishness. Selfish people often have so little sense of self-worth that they need to put themselves at center stage. To love ourselves means respecting ourselves, listening to inner hurts and longings, and bringing these to the Shepherd for healing and fulfillment.

We listen to our bodies—what they tell us of our needs, stress, and fatigue. Any guidance that teaches us to ignore or abuse our bodies or to neglect our general well-being is not the guidance of God's Holy Spirit. Both the Twenty-third Psalm and John 10 make clear the tender care of the Shepherd for the sheep.

The love whose welcome and reach extend over, through, and beyond all dividing walls is perhaps the supreme sign of guidance.

Reflection and Meditation

But now in Christ Jesus you who once were far off have been brought near. . . . For he is our peace . . . and has broken down the dividing wall. . . . So he came and pro-claimed peace to you who were far off and peace to those who were near.

—EPHESIANS 2:13-14, 17

Rest in whatever way feels best. Take a few slow, deep breaths, then breathe naturally. God enfolds you and longs to open you to widening love. When you feel ready, ask yourself the following questions:

- In my recent choices, are dividing walls going up or down between me and others?

- Does my spiritual community wall out anyone? If so, who? What form does the exclusion take?

- If recent decisions have resulted in this exclusion, what were those decisions? When were they made? Under what or whose influence?

- If my (our) choices have lowered these dividing walls, what brought about this change? What does the new inclusiveness feel like to me? Has it been painful? Has joy been involved? What other changes has it brought about in my life?

When you feel ready, ask God to open your awareness to other areas of exclusion in your life. Do any special thoughts or memories come?

If you feel ready to move into deeper meditation, take a deep, slow breath, then breathe naturally. Think of someone you find hard to understand or accept for some reason.

Picture or just think of this person sitting with you at the table of the Last Supper. Is this person sitting next to you, across the table, or at the other end? Accept what you feel.

The bread is broken by Jesus and passed from hand to hand around the table. Does it feel all right to eat of the same bread with this person? The cup is filled by Jesus and passed from hand to hand. How does it feel to drink from the same cup as this person?

If all this feels hard or even impossible, don't push yourself into other feelings. Tell Jesus how you feel. It is enough for now that you are in the same room with this person and at the same table. You can come back as often as you want. No one condemns you; you are being healed.

Now think of a part of your own self that feels unlovely or unacceptable to you or a part of yourself you do not understand. Picture or just think of Jesus bringing the bread and the cup to that "person" who is a part of you. Or perhaps Jesus anoints that inner person with healing oil. Take time to rest in this image or thought for as long a period as you feel it is helpful.

Then, when you feel ready, stretch, breathe deeply, and gently end your meditation.

Peace at Our Center

~

*My sheep listen to my voice; I know them, and they fol-
low me. I give them eternal life . . . ; no one can snatch
them out of my hand. My Father, who has given them to
me, is greater than all; no one can snatch them out of my
Father's hand.*

—JOHN 10:27-29, NIV

About thirty years ago, I was caught in one of those painful
dilemmas that we all face sooner or later. This was a particu-
larly rough one. Should I agree to a plan lovingly prepared for
a long time by people who were dear to me? Or, heeding warning signs in my health and strength and other serious obstacles,
should I say no?

I said no, quite definitely. The hurt went deep and lasted
for years, especially for two people I loved. The worst motives
were attributed to me. My good faith was questioned. It was

useless to try to talk it through. The misunderstanding was too deep, and the gulf opened between us was too great.

But I learned something during this painful time that has always stayed with me. In the midst of the emotional storm and stress, I experienced a powerful sense of safety and peace, of being held and companioned.

When we are under God's guidance we experience a center core of peace. On the night of his betrayal and arrest, Jesus said to his disciples as they shared their last supper together: "Peace I leave with you; my peace I give to you. I do not give to you as the world gives" (John 14:27).

Peace. It is a word we hear often in our Christian circles, and yet how often it is misunderstood. We often confuse peace with passivity, a passionless "peace at any price" way of relating that fears necessary confrontation and firmly setting borders and limits. Some people consider peace the same as resignation, a listless "whatever" attitude to the force that most dominates a situation. They may believe they are obeying God's will in this attitude.

Peace is certainly not the absence of caring, longing, passionate involvement, grief, or anger. We need to be suspicious of spiritualities that teach living in detachment from our human emotions, abandoning strong feelings. I believe that kind of approach dehumanizes us. Certainly we want to be healed of obsessive dependence on our wishes and longings. We don't want to get "stuck" in desires. But the way of the Incarnate One encourages us to bring forth our feelings, own them, listen to them, embrace them as part of ourselves. We ask God to heal feelings if they need healing and to let them become a part of our whole, transformed being.

Neither is peace the same as a stubborn, unmovable self-righteousness, which is closed off to the thoughts and feelings of others.

What then is peace? In the biblical sense, it means a wholeness and inner well-being (related to the Hebrew word *shalom*), and it also implies a specific empowering gift and blessing from God. Many biblical symbols represent this inner vibrant centeredness: the shining of a steady light; a deep, clear pool; a spring of water welling up and flowing forth from a profound source; a quiet word spoken to us in the center of the storm; firm rock beneath our feet; sheltering wings around us.

Years ago I read a true story, told by the woman who experienced it. Her husband had died suddenly, without warning, as they sat together in the living room early one evening. Hours later, after the ambulances, the doctors, the pastor, and the undertaker had come and gone, she sat alone in her home. Her grown-up children had been called and would fly in the next day. Her nearest neighbor was out of town. She didn't want strangers with her. She was alone that first night.

She was glad for her husband that he could die so quickly and painlessly. As for herself, she realized as she wandered around the quiet house that she was cold and shaking with shock. She could not bear to go up to their bedroom. She lay down on the sofa; inwardly, she reached out feebly to God for help. Instantly she felt herself enveloped from head to foot in deep, cradling warmth, just as if someone had come into the room and wrapped her in a thick feather quilt.

My mother called those feather quilts a comforter, she thought as she drifted off to sleep. *Jesus promised to send us the Holy Spirit, the Comforter. That must be what is enfolding me now.*

She knew that the word *Comforter* was an archaic term for the Holy Spirit, the Paraclete, more accurately translated as "advocate" or "guide." But it made no difference. That night it was bodily and emotional warmth and comfort she needed, and that was exactly the way God came to her. Indeed, the comfort she felt resembles Jesus' description of God holding the beloved sheep close and safe.

Comfort should not be confused with *comfortable*. This woman faced many hard, distressing tasks ahead, for which she would need courage, strength, and initiative. When God's Holy Spirit awakens radical new vision within us and calls us out to the risks of love, we will feel a profound inner stirring, often an impassioned response quite the opposite of comfortable. But at depth we are held, comforted.

What quality of inner peace came to Jesus when the angel ministered to him in Gethsemane, where he struggled in prayer? Was it the warmth and enfoldment that came to the woman on the night of her husband's death? Or was it the inner soaring of the spirit experienced by Habakkuk six hundred years earlier when he encountered invasion and tyranny?

> Though the fig tree does not blossom,
>   and no fruit is on the vines;
>
> . . . .
> yet will I rejoice in the LORD;
>
> . . . .
>   he . . . makes me tread upon the heights
>   (Hab. 3:17-19).

The Paraclete (the Greek word for Holy Spirit) literally means "the one who is called to our side," the one who stands by us. To me, this is none other than God's own self through the living Jesus Christ, the intimate, transforming presence. But this presence not only stands by our side as the deep Comforter but also calls us forth. "Shalom" (peace) was the first word the risen Jesus spoke to the disciples that Easter night. Then he breathed on them the vibrant power of the Holy Spirit and told them, "As the Father has sent me, so I send you" (John 20:21). All this was given before they even unlocked the door!

The *comfort* of the Presence was with the disciples and also the *power* to go forth. These two combined are the essence of that special quality of inner peace Christ gives. The steady quietness is not static but by nature moves forward. We are wrapped in warmth and also empowered to move.

An old hymn, not much sung these days, describes the quiet power of Christ's shalom, peace:

> They casts their nets in Galilee
> Just off the hills of brown;
> Such happy, simple fisherfolk,
> Before the Lord came down.
> Contented, peaceful fishermen,
> Before they ever knew
> The peace of God that filled their hearts
> Brimful, and broke them too.
>
> Young John who trimmed the flapping sail,
> Homeless, in Patmos died.
> Peter, who hauled the teeming net,
> Head down was crucified.
> The peace of God, it is no peace,
> But strife closed in the sod.
> Yet, brothers, pray for but one thing:
> The marvelous peace of God.
> ("They Cast their Nets" by William A. Percy)[1]

Provocative, disturbing words! But we understand their meaning when we think of times within our own guidance when we were deeply stirred, awakened, yet the still point within burned like a steady candle flame.

"Am I essentially at peace about my choice, about my life?" is a question of major priority to ask ourselves—and ask others. Not the so-called peace of resigned passivity or locked-in inflexibility. Not the absence of strong emotion or passionate conviction. Peace can underlie even rapidly pounding hearts. It can shine in the center even of anxiety and anger. It can dwell within intensity as the poised, unifying vision, able to be open, able to listen to others.

Lack of inner peace warns us to examine again our choices and explore our conflicts. The presence of inner peace is the still point of God, shining in those who walk the path of God's guidance.

Reflection and Meditation

No one will snatch them out of my hand. . . . no one can snatch them out of my Father's hand.

—JOHN 10:28-29, NIV

Relax your body in whatever way is best for you. Take a few slow, deep breaths, then breathe naturally. God's presence enfolds you. God hears your deep need. When you feel ready, reflect on these questions:

- Do I feel basic peace with my life, with my recent decisions?

- Is there an inner steadiness, calm, and comfort, even in the midst of outer conflict and turmoil or anxiety?

- Though I feel strongly about an issue, am I able to listen fully to others?

- What is my body telling me about my life, my recent choices? Does it feel dull and lethargic? tensed up most of the time? How is my health? Am I more vulnerable to accidents and infections? Is it hard to take deep, slow breaths?

- Think of a time when you made what turned out to be the right choice. What was the inner feeling at the time? How did your body feel? Do you feel this way now?

Relax again; again breathe slowly and deeply without pushing. Then breathe naturally.

What does inner peace feel like for you?

a deep central steadiness?

a quiet pool?

a spring of water flowing from the deep earth?

an inner light or star?

a color?

a sense of warmth?

a circle of light around you?

strong rock under your body?

wings or arms enfolding you?

a hand holding you?

a Presence with you?

a quiet word spoken deep within you?

a deep-rooted tree?

a bodily focusing?

rhythmic breathing?

a quiet candle flame?

an inner note or sound?

Chapter Nine

Hold your inner image, word, or feeling in your attentive heart. Does this feel like a reality for you now?

Turn to Christ's Holy Spirit which stands by you, guides you, prays in you and through you. What do you sense you are being told about your choices, your life?

When you feel ready, take a deep, quiet breath. Stretch; then gently massage your face and hands. Leave your meditation quietly.

God's Guidance in Our Churches and Spiritual Relationships

~

$\mathcal{I}$n chapter 3 I described a spiritual group that could have damaged my life, a group that in spite of its idealism and sincerity was directing me away from God's true guidance. I have also described another group whose incredibly releasing and empowering love influences me still, more than fifty years later. Looking back, I marvel at the giftedness of the second group's leaders.

In Jesus' name those leaders listened to members' dreams; encouraged our questions; rejoiced in our gifts and spontaneity; set us free to laugh, sing, play, pray, explore; and challenged us to love others and set them free. For decades this church student group influenced the lives of hundreds of young people. Jesus' living spirit was present in this communal body, healing and transforming far beyond what any one individual could do.

Jesus was always aware of the living soul of a communal body. He knew that every community had its own story, its wounds, its gifts, its incredible power over the lives of its members whether for good or destruction.

When Jesus would heal an individual, he was also keenly aware of the community from which that person came. He longed to heal not only that particular person but also the communal group that had shaped him or her. For example, when he healed the bent woman on the sabbath day, he longed not only to release her from her bodily bondage but also to release her whole village from the deeper spiritual bondage of putting rules and traditions ahead of compassion (Luke 13:10-17).

Sometimes Jesus did caution those he healed not to talk about their healing immediately to others. Perhaps he knew those particular persons needed more time for quiet reflection. But his healings and teachings were never esoteric, intended for the favored few. Everybody was welcome to listen; all were welcome to enter: "Nothing is covered up that will not be uncovered, and nothing secret that will not become known. What I say to you in the dark, tell in the light" (Matt. 10:26-27). Jesus understood his transforming spirit would work in communal bodies as well as in individual persons, as yeast expands in the dough.

A church or spiritual group discerns God's guidance through the same shining signs that are offered to individuals. What would attending to those signs mean in a practical way for communal discernment?

Recognizing the characteristics of the true Shepherd. The

foundation of a Christian group is the living Jesus Christ. If we turn away from this foundation, this living core of our life, we may still be a group with ideals, morals, inspirational thoughts, and friendly people, but we have lost our fire, our wind, our salt, our yeast. I visited such a church once. It was a beautiful building, full of friendly, nice people. The sermon consisted mainly of quotes from ancient and modern sages. The sanctuary contained no cross. No one mentioned Jesus. It was a pleasant gathering of neighbors, but a church? The transforming flame was not there. There was a curious emptiness at the center.

Let us not only talk *about* but talk *to* that healing, life-giving, life-changing Personality at our center. Let us witness to one another that Jesus walks among us, embraces us in our gatherings, touching our individual needs as well as our community's vaster, deeper needs. Let us remember that Jesus not only prayed for us at the Last Supper, but he still prays for us, with us, and within us.

Let us as a community keep reminding ourselves what Jesus is really like—a spirit of release, not rigidity; love that is pervasive, not invasive. Jesus invites us to relationship, not rules; calls us to communion, not conquest; offers bonding, not bondage. Jesus is a healer, not a destroyer; Jesus is life-giving, not condemning.

Called by name. Every community has its own unique identity and personality. What is best for *this* particular community, not just communities as a category? What is the history of this group, its wounds, its gifts? Has it experienced betrayal, loss of trust, schism? If this group were one person, what would it look like? How would it look if it spoke and told us its story, and in what way would it speak? Does it seem to have a spirit of anger? frustration? grieving? repression? silence? anxiety? a closed-off attitude? fragmentation? hurt? Or does it have a spirit of warmth, openness, strength?

It might be beneficial for a group within the community to share together their sense about the soul of the larger communal body. Participants may write a dialogue with the communal soul or draw what they perceive. Such a small gathering could pray for the communal soul, picturing the Healer embracing, healing, and transforming this communal soul.

Set free from intrusion and compulsion. A community needs periodically to ask its members if any form of invasion of freedom or coercive or manipulative practices are occurring. The following discerning questions may be used:

- Does any teaching or guidance make members feel anxious, pushed, or dominated? Do teachings make some members feel superior to others?

- Are questions and concerns truly heard? Are alternative viewpoints respected? How does the community handle dissent? Is the group expected to be passive, obedient?

- Is the community guided by guilt and shame? Are members singled out for criticism and reproof? pushed into commitments?

- Are group members extremely dependent on the leaders? Are the leaders accountable to any larger supervisory fellowship? Is there any "court of appeal" other than the leaders themselves?

- Are the leaders elitist, arrogant? Do they expect special privileges? Do they show concern and compassion for the members?

- Is the community sensitive to the hurts and reserve of the members? Do members explicitly have permission not to participate in any group activity? Are people pressured to share? Is there a sense of group satisfaction when a member has been pushed to break down, weep, confess all, surrender to the group? That would suggest the group finds emotional fulfillment in the collapse of a member.

- Are members allowed to bully, push, or dominate one another?

- Are members experiencing an unusual amount of sickness, depression, or addiction? Is there a loss of spontaneity, humor, closeness, and flexible openness?

Group leaders, whether pastors, chaplains, teachers, counselors, spiritual directors, or lay leaders, may ask themselves these questions:

- Do I respect each person's right to choose freely, even though I may disagree? Am I willing to release others to their own way and choices?

- Do I feel anger or anxiety if I am questioned or resisted? What is my body telling me about my inner reactions at such times?

- Am I able to listen with full attention to another person? Or am I preoccupied with my own opinion, my own agenda, or my own perfect theological, spiritual, or psychological answer?

- Do I try to fix another's problem immediately, or do I allow a space of silence for reflection? Do I interrupt a lot, or do I give space for the other to finish a thought?

- Do I ever push or manipulate others "for their own good"?

- When in consultation with another, am I also trying to listen to God's Spirit—open to learn and be changed?

- Am I willing and able to set borders in spiritual relationships to avoid draining, invasion of time, energy, and privacy as well as inappropriate mutual dependence?

- Do I remember that God through the living Christ is the source of all life and healing, that I am a living branch of that living Vine? Do I try to remain daily rooted and grounded in the living Vine?

An open gate before us. What actual problems face this particular community? What are the realities of the problem? Has the community actually prayed about the choices, not in a pro forma way but with depth listening and silence for reflection?

Some churches and spiritual groups make it a practice, even in business sessions, to take five minutes out of every half hour of discussion for silent prayer and reflection. (The responsibility for the stopwatch is passed around.) When the conversation resumes, a profoundly different attitude prevails, a deeper clarity *and* charity than before the silence. I have been present at such sessions and can witness to the release and power of this approach.

In this atmosphere of expectancy we can discern together what new thoughts, ideas, and visions are emerging. What possibilities are actually opening up? What old ways are diminishing in importance and priority? What new ways are appearing among us? What resources do we actually have in our communal body to match these visions? If the resources are not at present with us, do we push or do we pray?

Green pastures of our hearts. A communal body needs rest and a sense of fulfillment and renewal no less than individuals.

- Is our church, our group, actually experiencing God's abundance of sustenance, nurture, renewal?

- What is the level of basic well-being among our members? Do most of us both look and feel stressed and exhausted in our community work? Are there an unusual number of health problems, depression, breakdowns, addictions, family difficulties, in the community?

- Is there a sense of joy and warm fellowship along with the hard work? Do we see any fruitful results from the work, or do we seem to constantly face blocks and frustrations? Is our work accomplished mainly as a result of pushing and willpower, or do we feel a communal sense of empowerment flowing from God?

- Is there a lot of talk about sacrifice and self-denial as members of the body of Christ? Or is the emphasis on the abundance and joy that flow forth when we offer our lives to God?

- Does our church or spiritual group encourage members to ignore or neglect the needs and claims of families, daily work and responsibilities, bodily and emotional health? Or are we helped to recognize the possibilities for deep and transforming ministry within our ordinary daily lives and commitments?

- As a group, do we have fun together, times of refreshment and relaxation? Do we help one another discover our true longings, our true gifts? Or do we push unsuitable jobs on others or ourselves out of a sense of duty?

- In short, as a community in Christ, are we experiencing the inner abundant life Jesus promised us?

Love more inclusive. I recently visited a small, family-type church in a lovely woodsy setting. The beautiful little building, inspired choir, and excellent preacher made me believe this was a church of which anyone would be proud to be a member. At the end of the service no one spoke to me, though I was obviously a visitor in this small congregation. I walked up and down the aisle a few times and did receive a few quickly averted glances as people hurried by to greet their friends. Finally I went downstairs for the coffee gathering and stood unnoticed for quite a while. Eventually one couple did come up, and we had a brief, nice chat. This was my first and only greeting.

Why didn't I just introduce myself, take the initiative? Ordinarily I would have done so, especially in a large congregation where members genuinely might not know I was a stranger. But this blatant exclusion fascinated me. I decided to observe how far it would go. When I left, I wondered what had happened in this apparently beautiful household of God which led it to wall off strangers from welcome? Did decades of self-satisfaction and ingrown tradition simply prevent *seeing* the stranger in its midst?

Even more insidious than such *outer* exclusion is the *inner* spiritual exclusion that can occur even in churches where strangers are greeted. A community with an exclusive heart opens itself genuinely only to those whose clothes, opinions, or lifestyle conform to its own expectations.

In our communities under the guidance of the Shepherd, we need to ask ourselves regularly:

- Are we as a group urged to avoid or be suspicious of outsiders and their influence? We need to ask, Who are the Samaritans, the eunuchs, the tax collectors, the hemorrhaging ones, of our time and culture? Do we have church laws excluding them in any way? Do we have subtler ways of closing people out?

- What sorts of people are elected to positions of leadership? What type of person is asked to join and lead committees? Do we value theological correctness or practical skills more than loving warmth?

- Do invisible walls surround us, exclusions and restrictions not written in the books? If Jesus walked in our doors, sat in our pews (which, of course, he does), what would he see?

Peace at our center. Do we experience basic peace in our community? If not, we may question whether we are led by Christ's Spirit.

Communal peace is discerned on two levels. First, is the group essentially a peaceful place? Do people have a sense of enough time and space? Is there time to pray and reflect amidst all the business? Is there time for quiet sharing and conversation along with efficient scheduling? Symptoms of lack of peace include a rushed, overworked, overorganized sense of breathlessness and hurry. Urgent deadlines dominate the foreground. A push for perfectionism causes stress, guilt, and fatigue. Remember that "peace" does not imply lack of feelings and strong conviction; nor does it suggest a group is somnolent—that nothing is happening.

Another equally significant level for discerning peace is to examine whether either constant bickering and criticism or passive quiescence characterize the group. Either condition indicates peace is missing. Too often peace is misunderstood as absence of challenge, disagreement, or even confrontation. Too often, in the name of peace, we hesitate to bring up disturbing issues. We remain silent, sweeping the debris of years back under the rug where it silently pollutes the spiritual atmosphere. But honest disagreement or loving confrontation are not the same as harping criticism.

God's peace, as indicated in the previous chapter, can exist even in the midst of open, deep differences. This is the peace founded on that vision of Isaiah in which all the different animals dwell together on God's holy mountain, in God's shalom. They live in peace not because they are alike, which they definitely are not, but because they care as much about one another's uniqueness and integrity as they do about their own. God's peace never reduces us to one type, one opinion, one substance. God does something far more exciting, creating us increasingly *various*. Instead of boring homogeneity, our peace is risky polarity. The church is the special crucible where this fantastic miracle is supposed to take place.

Does this vision of dynamic peace and risky polarity ask too much of human beings? Probably, if we depended on our good intentions and willpower. But we are not asked to depend on ourselves. We are to open ourselves daily to Christ's transforming Holy Spirit, which brings this miraculous way of living together into being.

In practical ways, what does being open to transformation mean? It means we take intentional time for silent reflection and prayer at intervals before, during, and after our meetings. We agree that only God has the perfect answer to our problems and choices; we need time for group listening to allow that answer to unfold. We help one another understand that critical bickering is *not* the same as open discussion about our disagreement. Challenge and disagreement can take place in an atmosphere of loving respect in spite of the almost inevitable tension. It means each member is honored and valued and that all opinions are to be thoroughly heard. No one is allowed to bully, shame, or push others in the name of conformity. We may leave a meeting still disagreeing with others but knowing that we all dwell together in God's embrace. It does not mean that we have to *like* each other but that inwardly we can say to the other (in the wonderful words I heard from a pastor some years ago), "Give me your blessing, child of God."

A communal body that falls under the domination of those who misguide—spiritual dictators, abusers, or the uncaring and uncommitted (whom Jesus called the "hired hands" in his story of sheep and shepherd)—or under the guidance of a rigid or predatory ideology can harm or even destroy the well-being of individuals for generations. But a communal body rooted and grounded in Christ's spirit of inclusive love, healing, and transformation will fulfill another of Isaiah's visions concerning healed and healing communities:

> They will be called oaks of righteousness,
>> the planting of the LORD, to display his glory.
> They shall build up the ancient ruins,
>> they shall raise up the former devastations;
> they shall repair the ruined cities,
>> the devastations of many generations (Isa. 61:3-4).

Chapter Ten

Meditation for Communal Discernment and Healing

Jesus came and stood among them and said, "Peace be with you." After he said this, he showed them his hands and his side. . . . Jesus said to them again, "Peace be with you. As the Father has sent me, so I send you." When he had said this, he breathed on them and said to them, "Receive the Holy Spirit."

—JOHN 20:19-22

NOTE: This meditation can be led by a group facilitator for the whole or a part of a community. Each individual participant is free at any time to withdraw from a particular meditation and enter into another form of prayer. Also, each is free to change or adapt imagings, metaphors, or wording.

Let us sit, lie down, or stand in a relaxed but open posture. God's love enfolds the communal body, and the living Jesus Christ is with us, praying with us, for us, and through us.

We can now take a few deep breaths, slowly and gently. Each breath is God's breath of life breathed upon us. As a community gathered in the name of Jesus, each breath we breathe is also Jesus' breath of the Holy Spirit upon us. Now breathe naturally.

Some of us may wish to rest quietly in God's healing presence. Others who feel ready are invited to think of a particular problem, choice, or decision the community faces. Despite whatever deep convictions and opinions we each may have, only God has the ultimate answer for the community. Rest in quietness and openness, giving thanks that God surrounds our community and will guide us.

Let us keep our bodies relaxed, our breathing calm and gentle, our hearts and minds open.

Think of or picture our community as if it were one person. How would this person look? What would be the expression on his or her face? Does this person seem hurt, angry, confused? What is the special need of this person? What is the main problem he or she is facing?

When ready, we can think of or picture the living Jesus Christ joining the person (the personified spirit of this community). What seems to happen? Does Christ the Healer talk quietly with this person? lay on healing hands? anoint with healing oil?

Some of us may prefer to think of this gathering surrounded by light, held in healing hands, or under sheltering wings. Some may wish to pray after this manner:

Loving God, here are your people, your children, gathered together open to you, waiting for your guidance. May Jesus, our Good Shepherd, become more real for us. May we begin to hear the Shepherd's voice in our hearts, and to feel the Shepherd's light around us. May the Shepherd's love increase among us and beyond us. May the Shepherd's peace abide in us. May the Shepherd's Spirit heal and transform us. We pray this in the power of the Shepherd's name.

Let each person come quietly out of the meditation, taking whatever time he or she needs. Some may wish to leave in silence. Others may wish to stay and greet one another.

Jesus, the Good Shepherd

~

I am the good shepherd.

—JOHN 10:11

Recently our daughter gave us a framed art photo featuring a mountain pinnacle of golden sandstone. On the summit stands a person surrounded with light, a crooked staff in hand, arms outstretched.

"That must be Moses, receiving the Ten Commandments," said one family member. "Or perhaps John the Baptist in the wilderness?"

"Oh no," said another. "It is obviously Jesus on the Mount of Transfiguration, just after his vision of Moses and Elijah."

"I don't see any of that," someone else said firmly. "All I see is a mountain climber with the sun at his back, waving at the photographer. But I admit he seems to be wearing a robe, and the shape of his stick *is* a bit odd."

None of these suggestions sounded quite right. We did not know, of course, what it signified to the photographer, but as with any work of art, the question was what did it say to *us*? Suddenly we knew. The realization came like thunder.

"Of *course*, that is Jesus in the desert of temptation. This is the moment when on the mountaintop he was offered all the kingdoms of the world. He has refused that false guidance. This must be the moment of choice when he becomes not the dictator of us all but the Shepherd of us all. At this moment the staff in his hand becomes the Shepherd's crook."

That is what the picture meant to our family. I am looking at it now as I write. What a fierce temptation it must have been for Jesus to take the world by storm, to bring the world's kingdoms forcibly under God's control. How quickly and completely he could have fed the poor and forced peace upon the nations. Even if it was a demonic temptation, wouldn't the results justify the means? He had the power; he felt it. It could be done. So many before and since have taken that road, dominating and enforcing in God's name. Inevitably corruption follows, corruption that already exists at the heart of dictatorship. If Jesus, with his incredible powers, had chosen that path, the cataclysmic results for us all would have been unimaginable.

Yes, he could have done it, but he would not. He chose the path of the lover, the suffering servant of us all. And at that moment, the Shepherd was among us.

Since we are set free by God to choose, we too experience our own wilderness of temptation. We too are offered the manipulative shortcuts, the uses of force and dominance. We too are invited to go under the guidance of powers that are not of God's Spirit.

Our temptations do not usually come with satanic faces. We have explored in this book the many varieties of misguidance rising from well-meaning but intrusive friends, family, and spiritual leaders as well as communal ideologies. We have experienced misguidance from the unhealed wounds within us, our unexpressed longings, our own emotional habits and rigid mind-sets. Often we have wandered off the path or guided others astray, thinking it was God's will.

Someone might read a book like this and feel depressed over the frequent instances he or she has mistaken or ignored the shining signs. Certainly during the book's writing, I have seen again the many ways I have intruded presumptuously on others and allowed others to intrude and misguide me.

But this I have learned: Christ's Holy Spirit does *not* lead us to self-contempt or to self-condemnation. There are many spirits that do condemn—including our own. But God's Spirit, though showing us the truth about ourselves, hastens at that same moment to comfort, restore, and to challenge and empower us again. No matter how far we may have wandered from true guidance, we never wander out of God's love. We have harmed ourselves and others, but never for a moment have we fallen out of God's hand.

God's hand. Recall the scripture verse we looked at in chapter 9 on inner peace: "No one will snatch them out of my hand. . . . no one can snatch them out of my Father's hand" (John 10:28-29, NIV). This is a hand that does not punish, a hand that does not squeeze us or crush us. We are held with infinite gentleness as well as great strength. Sometimes we may kick against it, ignore it, fall asleep in this hand. But we never fall out and are never dropped.

God's hand both holds us and empowers us, renewing our strength and confidence, those two great signs of the Holy

Spirit. Many years ago (on Mother's Day, of all "coincidences") soon after sunrise, our daughter found a young robin shivering in the grass in our garden. It was not a baby bird; it had all its feathers and was of an age to fly. But for some reason its wings were not strong enough. It could hop, but it could not fly. Apparently its parents had got impatient, pushed it out of the nest, and departed. They were nowhere to be seen. The bird crouched in the grass awaiting developments, which would not have been long delayed, for the neighborhood was full of cats!

I have never forgotten the way our daughter cupped her two hands beneath and around the trembling bird, lightly enough for it to breathe and flutter its wings but firmly enough so that it could not fall. *Those are God's hands*, I remember thinking. "Are not two sparrows sold for a penny? Yet not one of them will fall to the ground apart from your Father" (Matt. 10:29).

I thought again of God's hands as I watched her feeding and tending the bird for the next two weeks while it grew strong enough to fly. She would take it into the garden for short periods to try its wings and learn to avoid cats. Finally she released the bird in a nearby park. We watched it fly with joyful confidence into the trees and saw it no more. At this point there is an important difference between our hands and God's. When God holds, comforts, warms, feeds, and strengthens us so we may stretch our wings and fly, we will fly. But God will continue to undergird us with those infinite guiding hands:

> If I take the wings of the morning,
> and dwell in the uttermost parts of the sea;
> Even there shall thy hand lead me,
> and thy right hand shall hold me (Ps. 139:9-10, KJV).

But why am I thinking about birds when this book centers on the true Shepherd and the sheep? Because I know Jesus thought about birds. He knew all about those pathetic tiny sparrows sold two-for-a-penny in the market. As a boy, perhaps he had bought a sparrow in the market, brought it home, fed it, strengthened it until it could fly in freedom. As he watched it fly, did he think of the psalmist's words that no one flies beyond the circle of God's love, that no one will be abandoned by that guiding hand?

I again look at that photo of the figure bathed in light on the mountaintop. As Jesus made that supreme choice to become the lover of the world, did he watch the birds circling around him, flying in freedom, guided by love? Did he also see in the distance the homeless sheep searching for grass in the desert?

What else is he looking for on that great mountain pinnacle? Certainly he gazes no longer on the kingdoms of the world and their splendor, for now the staff in his hand has become the shepherd's crook. He looks for us. We have flown away; we have wandered off so often. Perhaps in our broken, mistaken choices we thought we had left God and God's guidance, never to return to that heart and those hands. But the Shepherd comes for us forever, especially when we have wandered off the path.

For that is what good shepherds do.

Notes

CHAPTER 5

1. Patricia Evans, *Controlling People: How to Recognize, Understand, and Deal with People Who Try to Control You* (Avon, Mass.: Adams Media Corp., 2002), 77.

CHAPTER 9

1. William A. Percy, "They Cast their Nets," in *Pilgrim Hymnal* (The Pilgrim Press, 1958), 340.

About the Author

FLORA SLOSSON WUELLNER has a specialized ministry of spiritual renewal and inner healing, offered to both individuals and communities. She is a teacher, retreat leader, spiritual director, and author. Wuellner is an ordained minister in the United Church of Christ and formerly adjunct faculty at the Pacific School of Religion in Berkeley, California.

Other Titles by
Flora Slosson Wuellner

from Upper Room Books

Feed My Shepherds: Spiritual Healing and Renewal for Those in Christian Leadership (0-8358-0845-9)

Forgiveness, the Passionate Journey: Nine Steps of Forgiving Through Jesus' Beatitudes (0-8358-0945-5)

Prayer and Our Bodies (0-8358-0568-9)

Prayer, Stress, and Our Inner Wounds (0-8358-0501-8)

Release: Healing from Wounds of Family, Church, and Community (0-8358-0775-4)

These books are available through your local
bookstore or you may order directly from
Upper Room Books
1-800-972-0433
online at www.upperroom.org